R. Hooper (signature)

BASIC EVALUATION METHODS

Glynis M. Breakwell
and
Lynne Millward

Personal and Professional Development

BASIC EVALUATION METHODS

Analysing performance, practice and procedure

Glynis M. Breakwell
and
Lynne Millward

BPS
BOOKS Published by The British Psychological Society

First published in 1995 by BPS Books (The British Psychological Society),
St Andrews House, 48 Princess Road East, Leicester LE1 7DR.

A catalogue record for this book is available from the British Library.

ISBN 1 85433 161 2 paperback

Typeset by Gem Graphics, Trenance, Mawgan Porth, Cornwall
Printed in Great Britain by BPC Wheatons Ltd, Exeter

Personal and Professional Development

SERIES EDITORS:

Glynis M. Breakwell is Professor of Psychology and Head of the Psychology Department at the University of Surrey.

David Fontana is Reader in Educational Psychology at University of Wales College of Cardiff, and Professor Catedrático, University of Minho, Portugal.

The books in this series are designed to help readers use psychological insights, theories and methods to address issues which arise regularly in their own personal and professional lives and which affect how they manage their jobs and careers. Psychologists have a great deal to say about how to improve our work styles. The emphasis in this series is upon presenting psychology in a way which is easily understood and usable. We are committed to enabling our readers to use psychology, applying it for themselves to themselves.

The books adopt a highly practical approach. Readers are confronted with examples and exercises which require them to analyse their own situation and review carefully what they think, feel and do. Such analyses are necessary precursors in coming to an understanding of where and what changes are needed, or can reasonably be made.

These books do not reflect any single approach in psychology. The editors come from different branches of the discipline. They work together with the authors to ensure that each book provides a fair and comprehensive review of the psychology relevant to the issues discussed.

Each book deals with a clearly defined target and can stand alone. But combined they form an integrated and broad resource, making wide areas of psychological expertise more freely accessible.

OTHER TITLES IN THE SERIES

Coaching for Staff Development by Angela Thomas
Effective Teamwork by Michael West
Interpersonal Conflicts at Work by Robert J. Edelmann
Managing Time by David Fontana

Contents

1. INTRODUCING EVALUATION   1
The structure and purpose of this book   1
What is evaluation?   2
What can be evaluated?   3
What are the purposes of evaluation?   4
Who does evaluation?   5
Self-evaluation   8
The costs and benefits of evaluation   11

2. WHEN TO EVALUATE   16
When should you do an evaluation?   16
Pointless evaluation: information, not intelligence   18
Evaluation before the event   20
Evaluating process or outcome   24
Evaluating complex, long-term or diffuse outcomes   25
Building evaluation into the initial design of targets   27
The ethics of evaluation   28

3. MAPPING THE STRATEGY: DESIGNING AN
   EVALUATION   31
Steps in designing an evaluation   31
Types of design   33
Optimize the design solution   40
Evaluation in retrospect   45

4. EVALUATION TACTICS: COLLECTING DATA AND
   IMPOSING MEASUREMENT   47
Evidence and the issue of measurement   47
Types of method   48
Observation   49
The observer and the observation situation   55
Asking questions   58

5. HANDLING EVALUATION INFORMATION:
   ANALYSIS OF DATA   77
The basic data handling model   78
Describing and summarizing data   80
Drawing inferences   83
Examples of data analysis   86
The issues of prediction and explanation   96

6. PRESENTING THE FINDINGS   98

Preparing to disseminate evaluation information   98
Differences between written and oral presentation   105
Managing the delivery of an oral presentation   108
Writing the report   115
Translating data: the use of visual media   118

7. PUTTING THE FINDINGS INTO PRACTICE   125

Problems in using evaluation findings   125
Bases of evaluator power   128
What can go wrong in putting findings into practice?   130
Self-evaluation and change   133
Resistance to organizational change   135
Conclusion: the rhetoric of evaluation   141

Exercise 1: The self-evaluation checklist   9
Exercise 2: An initial evaluation assessment   15
Exercise 3: Posing answerable questions   19
Exercise 4: Case study: a planning exercise   103
Exercise 5: Making an effective presentation   113
Exercise 6: Writing a report summary   117
Exercise 7: Translating data into graphic form   124
Exercise 8: How good are you at listening to yourself?   134

To Vera Breakwell

Chapter One

Introducing Evaluation

THE STRUCTURE AND PURPOSE OF THIS BOOK

Anyone who may be considering doing an evaluation or who is being subjected to an evaluation by others will find this book useful. It is designed for a broad range of people who may need to know about evaluation methods but whose professional training might not have included such skills; for instance, practitioners in the health and social services, educationalists, providers of cultural or leisure facilities (such as libraries or museums, theatre or sports centres) or managers in industrial, commercial or financial companies.

The purpose of the book is to introduce the reader to the basic methods used in evaluation studies. After describing what evaluation techniques can offer, the book explains when they can and should be used. It summarizes how to plan an evaluation and the range of tactics that can be used to collect relevant information. This is followed by an outline of some of the most frequently used procedures for making sense and drawing inferences from the data generated by evaluations. Understanding how to analyse evaluation data is the key to producing valid conclusions but this must be complemented by an ability to present the findings in a way that is suited to the target audience. Consequently, the book explores the factors which need to be taken into account when reporting the results of an evaluation.

Evaluations are rarely conducted as an end in themselves. They are done mostly in order to assess the need for change and, sometimes, to determine the viability of particular forms of change. It is therefore important in a book like this to explore how the results of evaluation can be used to promote and shape change.

This book is not written for experts in evaluation methods, (though for them it may be useful as a reference text, nevertheless). Primarily, it is a starting point for those who are interested in learning about evaluation methods. It provides essential information for anyone about to embark on an evaluation, or for those trying to understand the implications of an evaluation conducted by someone else. It is a practical guide rather than a comprehensive, academic text. No prior research experience on the part of the reader is assumed. However, anyone familiar with the design and statistical analysis of research will see evident parallels between scientific models of social research and the principles of evaluation described. It will be helpful to have some background knowledge of such scientific models but this is not essential.

The book uses a combination of straightforward information presentation, self-assessment and practical exercises; case study examples allow readers to progress to a point where it is possible for them to design, execute, and analyse an evaluation and then use it as the foundation for deciding about the need for change. However, evaluation is fraught with difficulties, both technical and ethical, and a significant part of this book is devoted to identifying these problems and illustrating how they can be solved, minimized or avoided.

WHAT IS EVALUATION?

Evaluation methods are distinguishable from other research methods in terms of their purpose, which is to establish whether specified activities, systems and physical arrangements are effective. They are used to assess how far certain provisions, practices or procedures (what might be called 'the three Ps') are actually achieving the objectives set for them. Evaluations may, on occasion, go further and attempt to establish why objectives are not achieved by the three Ps. Evaluation is therefore quite different from an auditing process. Auditing tells you what is happening; it is essentially descriptive. Evaluation tells you whether what is happening is producing the results that you want; it is primarily analytic.

Evaluation techniques are essential tools of management practice today. No professional can afford not to take an analytic approach to the job to be done. Evaluation is the first step towards improving your own performance and the performance of others – the precursor to maximizing effectiveness, the mechanism for minimizing ineffectiveness.

In principle, evaluation is an objective process. It should be designed carefully to exclude subjective biases and to ensure valid and reliable results. However, the pursuit of evaluation has acquired a rather bad reputation. It has come to be seen as a political and economic tool. Cynics have argued that evaluation is often now used merely as a means of rationalizing decisions which have already been taken and which usually involve redundancy, service reduction or increased productivity. It is undoubtedly true that evaluation is open to such misuse and it is unlikely that this will ever be eradicated completely. We believe that one way to minimize misuse is to educate a broader range of people about how legitimate evaluations may be conducted. We would argue that as more people become familiar with evaluation principles and methods it will become much more difficult to use evaluations to mislead or control them.

Of course, evaluation is not always a Machiavellian trick. It is, nevertheless, essentially a two-edged sword. For at the same time that it shows the value of a provision, practice, or procedure, evaluation will also lay bare the weaknesses. It may be vital to use evaluation to prove the merits of a set of activities but the process is also likely to reveal the inadequacies of these activities. When embarking upon an evaluation it is important to recognize the likely costs as well as the potential benefits. Any evaluation should be obliged to bear the warning 'user beware'.

WHAT CAN BE EVALUATED?

Evaluation tactics are now so diverse that it is feasible to evaluate virtually anything. It is possible to categorize the types of things which can be evaluated broadly as follows:

1. *Activity* – The impact of anything ranging from a single act to an entire repertoire of activity; exhibited by an individual or produced by several different people.

2. *Personnel* – The relevance and adequacy of the ability or skills of the people engaged in the task.

3. *Provision of resources* – The availability of the physical arrangements, space, equipment, 'person power' and money necessary for the task.

4. *Organizational structure* – The viability in the context of the task of the existing leadership practices, team formations and dynamics, communication channels, training regimes, and so on.

5. *Objectives* – The appropriateness of the goals which have been established; usually this includes an examination of the rationale for their timetable.

Where an evaluation encompasses all or most of these targets, it is sometimes referred to as a 'programme evaluation'. Where this term is used in the book, therefore, this generic definition is intended. The term 'programme evaluation' has, however, taken on a rather more specific meaning more recently. It is frequently used to refer to those major programmes, developed mainly in the US, to assess the impact of large-scale social policy interventions. For instance, programme evaluation has been used to examine the impact of racial desegregation in education. There is nothing magical or different about the methods which are used in this sort of programme evaluation. The difference lies in the scale of the data collection rather than in the philosophy or techniques.

Each of the five targets listed above involves the evaluation of people at some level. Even where the assessment ostensibly focuses solely upon procedures or organizational structure, it will inevitably examine the role of the people executing those procedures, the individuals inhabiting the structure.

WHAT ARE THE PURPOSES OF EVALUATION?

There are three fundamental reasons for conducting an evaluation:

1. *To validate* – Evaluation may be used to validate in the sense that it is the basis for gaining acceptance for the status quo and for resisting change. In this context it is actually being used to justify or defend what currently happens.

2. *To improve* – Evaluation may set out to improve existing provisions, practices or procedures. It can pursue this purpose even where it is acknowledged that what is happening now is worthwhile; it is simply believed that things could be better.

3. *To condemn* – Evaluation can be designed to condemn existing practice. The objective in this case is not necessarily to find out what would be better but to prove that what is done now is inadequate.

Validation, improvement and condemnation are quite distinct reasons for conducting an evaluation. The reason which motivates an evaluation will have an influence on how it is conducted, affecting design, analysis and the presentation of findings – issues which will be explored in later chapters.

The reason why an evaluation is conducted will be linked also to the stage that a given target has reached in its life-style. Of course, targets vary in their longevity. Some targets are fixed, short-term, one-off occurrences. For example, a health education campaign lasting one month to highlight the negative effects of a pregnant woman's smoking on her foetus would fall into this category. Some targets are continuous and have no fixed time limit: for instance, working arrangements to ensure high productivity on an assembly line. Some targets are iterative or recycled: for instance, structured therapeutic interventions used with different clients over time. It is therefore not a straightforward matter to talk about the life-cycle of the target. But something like a tripartite distinction of stages in the life-cycle might be valid: planning and start up; operational; and decommissioning. The reason for an evaluation in the first stage is most likely to be validation. In the second stage it is likely to be improvement. By the final stage, the primary reason for evaluation will be condemnation.

WHO DOES EVALUATION?

Evaluation is now big business. Organizations have realized that appropriate programme evaluation can improve operations (and consequently increase profits), and are willing to pay professionals to provide them. Firms offering evaluation consultancy are multiplying. Yet evaluation by an external or independent agent is only one of the models which can be adopted. With the right guidance anyone can conduct an evaluation. By the end of this book you will be introduced to all the necessary concepts and skills.

Remember, what is evaluated always has some human element. Where the target for evaluation has a very limited human component, the salience of the relationship between the evaluated and evaluator in determining design and analytic approaches will obviously decline.

The different types of relationship between the evaluator and the evaluated are summarized in the Box on page 7. Given these three independent dimensions it is possible to construct eight different types of potential relationships between the evaluator and the evaluated:

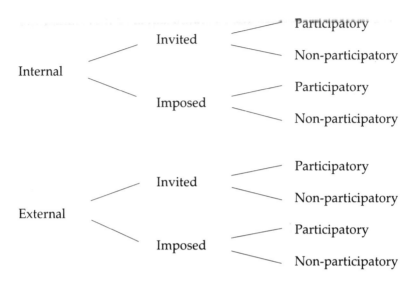

Each type has its own advantages and disadvantages. The nature of the relationship affects many aspects of the evaluation process. It may affect:

- the definition of the target for evaluation
- the access to information
- the validity and reliability of information gathered
- the relevance of recommendations
- the potential for change following evaluation
- the willingness to accept the findings of the evaluation
- the ethical status of the study.

For instance, a participatory relationship often results in the collection of more subtle and pertinent information; but this may be biased by lack of objectivity. Or, for example, the imposed evaluation may have a clear and appropriate definition of the criteria against which a team's activity is to be tested but can be subverted because people will not co-operate in answering questions. The external evaluation may be conducted with great expertise but, through lack of local knowledge, may miss key information and lack credibility.

THE RELATIONSHIP BETWEEN EVALUATOR AND EVALUATED

There are a number of dimensions along which the relationship between evaluator and evaluated can be described:

INTERNAL–EXTERNAL

The internal–external dimension refers to the person (or people) conducting the evaluation. If conducted by a group of people who are part of the organization which is being evaluated, the evaluation would be considered internal. Obviously, in large, complex organizations this distinction between insiders and outsiders is not always clear cut. Often, big organizations will be so sub-divided that different sections treat each other as alien; in this situation evaluation which is conducted across the sub-divisions will be regarded as external.

INVITED–IMPOSED

The invited–imposed dimension refers to those who decide that the evaluation shall be conducted. This dimension operates at a number of levels. Evaluation can be regarded as necessary by the management of an organization and then imposed upon their work-force: a form of internal imposition. Evaluation can be required of an organization by outside agencies (e.g. government, financial sponsors, etc): a form of external imposition. Of course, on occasion, evaluation can be recognized by more or less all concerned in the organization as timely and useful. In these circumstances, the evaluation would be considered consensually invited. Less frequently, evaluation will be invited by the work-force who wish to use it to improve working conditions.

PARTICIPATORY–NON-PARTICIPATORY

The participatory–non-participatory dimension refers to how far the evaluated are involved in the process of designing and interpreting the evaluation. In fact, evaluations can be conducted in such a way that those being

- *continued* -

continued –

> evaluated are never aware (until they are faced with the results) that any study is occurring. For instance, the success and/or efficiency of a social service operation can be assessed using secondary sources of information (such as statistics on number of clients seen) and the individuals, whose work is evaluated, need never know that the assessment has taken place. Increasingly, evaluations use sophisticated meta-analyses described in Chapter 2 which allow for 'silent' assessments.

SELF-EVALUATION

Individuals can conduct meaningful evaluations of their own activities using fundamentally the same principles of evaluation that are used in the more complex or wide-ranging studies. The difference lies in the scale of the operation rather than in the factors which must be considered, though there are some modifications in tactics.

Below is a short checklist (see *Exercise 1*) which is designed to tell you whether it is likely that you need to conduct a self-evaluation of your activities. The self-evaluation checklist is geared to your activities in the course of your work but you could apply it to your domestic situation or even your leisure activities.

Exercise 1 is simply a way of summarizing the reasons why you might want to self-evaluate. Knowing your own objectives, knowing whether you are achieving them efficiently and knowing if they could be attained in some other way is important and self-evaluation will allow you to acquire such knowledge. If you are constrained by legal requirements and/or have clear accountability for your actions (for instance to clients), self-evaluation provides valuable evidence of appropriate performance but also evidence that you treat your obligations seriously. Self-evaluation can also be very useful in the diagnosis of problems, particularly if you are vaguely aware that things are not going quite as they should but are unable to locate the reason. Self-evaluation data can be used to support a case for greater recognition and reward where you feel you are undervalued. Perhaps most importantly, self-evaluation can remove your own doubts about how well you are doing and how others are reacting to you.

THE SELF-EVALUATION CHECKLIST

EXERCISE 1

First, choose an area of your activities which you might consider evaluating. The size or range of the area is up to you. It could be a single activity. It could be a complex parcel of activities (for example, your working life). In answering the questions, keep this single area of activities in mind.

Warning: you may have difficulty answering these questions if you are unable to specify the objectives at which the activity is aimed. If this occurs, it is fairly safe to say that you need to engage in a self-evaluation anyway. If you are doing something for reasons which you cannot identify, it is probably time to evaluate that activity.

Answer the following questions by placing a tick as appropriate in the 'yes' or 'no' column.

In this area of your activity . . .	**YES**	**NO**
A. Is it important to you that you achieve your objectives?	☐	☐
B. Does it matter to you whether you achieve your objectives efficiently?	☐	☐
C. Are you constrained by legal requirements?	☐	☐
D. Are you accountable to other people?	☐	☐
E. Do you know whether you are performing well?	☐	☐
F. Are you aware of how the people affected by your activity react to it?	☐	☐
G. Do you think you have any problems for which you have no answers yet?	☐	☐
H. Do you think you may be wasting effort but do not know why?	☐	☐
J. Is what you do properly rewarded in your opinion?	☐	☐
K. Have you examined alternative ways of achieving your objectives?	☐	☐

How to score points
Score one point for each answer of 'yes' to questions A, B, C, D, G, and H. Score one point for each answer of 'no' to questions E, F, J and K. Total your score. The higher your score, the greater the need for you to conduct a self-evaluation.

Any one of these reasons might be sufficient in itself for you to feel that you need to do some self-evaluation. Their relative importance is a question of individual values and concerns. So, a low score on the checklist will not necessarily mean that you are uninterested in self-evaluation. However, a high score almost certainly means that you should be. Having done the checklist for one area of your activities, you might like to try it on another quite different type of activity. This might help you to sharpen your thinking about the potential disparities between different areas of your activities.

There is one further point to consider here. Self-evaluations, like other forms of evaluation, can be one-off events, spasmodically repeated, or continuous i.e. built into the programme of activities themselves. In assessing whether self-evaluation is worthwhile, it is also appropriate to consider what form it should take. The approach chosen will depend on the relative costs and benefits incurred. The section on the costs and benefits of evaluation later in this chapter sets out some of the factors which should be considered.

SELF-EVALUATION AND THE APPRAISAL PROCESS

Of course, it may occur to you, having done the self-evaluation checklist, that it is not you who should be considering the need for self-evaluation but someone else with whom you work. The checklist can be useful to anyone who is directing or managing the work of other people as a tool in the appraisal process. The appraiser can ask the appraisee to answer these questions and consider the implications of their responses as part of the appraisal process. In fact, the checklist includes some questions which focus especially upon the way someone is performing their job. As part of the appraisal process, this reflection upon the possible need for evaluation can be a useful catalyst. It encourages people to think about the possibility of, and reasons for, change. Used systematically by an appraiser, the checklist may provide data that can then be used as the basis for targeting subsequent evaluation studies.

Self-evaluation is sometimes included as an integral part of the appraisal process. Often the self-evaluation required is unstructured and varies according to the people appraised. However, it can be guided by an employer and become fairly standardized. In this type of self-evaluation, you collect your own data about your own performance and impact but the choice of what data you collect is constrained in that it is determined, at least to some extent, by someone else. In effect, you become a sort of research assistant *and* a subject in the research simultaneously. This type of self-evaluation is then usable as part of an organizational pro-gramme of evaluation that can be attached to appraisal.

It is clearly necessary to distinguish between the self-evaluation which an individual may conduct spontaneously, under no duress, and that required by an employer or some other authority. Even if the information collected is the same and leads to the same identified need for change, the individual involved will relate differently. The motivation for the self-evaluation is different and the ownership of the outcomes is different. Similarly, the emotions aroused will be different. Where self-evaluation is conducted as part of a wider programme, it can be classified as 'internal', 'imposed', and 'participatory' in terms of the dimensions described earlier.

THE COSTS AND BENEFITS OF EVALUATION

The potential costs and benefits of doing an evaluation are sum-marized in the Box on page 12. Not all the factors listed will be pertinent to your situation but before embarking upon any evalua-tion it is sensible to go through the list and check whether, in the case that you have in mind, the benefits are likely to outweigh the costs. You should examine how far each of these costs and benefits can be quantified – that is, given a value or significance.

For some, such as the estimate of financial outlay, quantification may be relatively easy, but for others, like the arousal of anxiety, putting some numerical value on the cost is impossible. This exercise of weighing costs and benefits will always involve value judgements. It is also coloured by expectations (or guesses) about the likely outcomes of the evaluation. The fact that the assessment of costs and benefits will be imprecise should not deter you from doing it, however. It is particularly important to consider thoroughly the arguments against the evaluation before you start. These arguments are bound to arise in the course of the evaluation and you need to know what you think about them and have ready your own counter-arguments.

Of course, this list can be used by anyone facing an imposed evaluation to help organize an assessment of why the evaluation is being done and how it may be shown to be either necessary or superfluous. The same considerations which determine whether to conduct an evaluation should also be borne in mind when deciding whether to attack or undermine it. This comment is not designed to be cynical but it must be recognized that the costs and benefits of an evaluation study will depend very much upon where you

---

THE COSTS AND BENEFITS OF EVALUATION

COSTS
entails financial outlay
incurs opportunity penalties (doing this means not doing
    something else)
arouses distrust and anxiety
might yield unanticipated and unwelcome results
makes you aware of problems that are impossible to solve
provides ammunition for enemies
heightens internal competition
instigates external and internal opposition
initiates unrealistic expectations about change
involves penalties if findings are ignored or misconstrued.

BENEFITS
estimates strengths, weaknesses, opportunities and
    constraints
aids quality assurance
makes it evident that you are taking accountability
    seriously
specifies where you are succeeding
identifies problems and suggests solutions to them
justifies change already planned
allows change to be monitored
erects standards for future assessments
refines objectives for the future
improves credibility of basis for case for extra resources
heightens staff motivation, if sometimes only temporarily.

NOTE: Not all costs and all benefits will be associated with every evaluation study. Each evaluation will have a unique pattern of costs and benefits associated with it. Anticipating what they will be is part of the task of any good evaluator.

stand in relation to the process and its likely implications. The costs and benefits will be viewed quite differently by different people involved in the same process. To some extent anticipating how others involved in the process will assess its value is important because it allows you to anticipate how they will react and this may be important in determining whether the evaluation works well or not.

THE SOCIAL SERVICES TEAM: A CASE STUDY IN THE COSTS AND BENEFITS OF EVALUATION

In order to gain insight into how costs and benefits can be calculated, it is useful to consider a case study in evaluation. While this particular example is drawn from social services operations, however, there are obvious parallels in both the health and the education services.

The manager of a team of social workers was considering whether it was appropriate to evaluate the adequacy of the service provided by her staff to the elderly within the community. To begin with, this manager was encouraged to do a systematic assessment of the costs and benefits involved in the proposed evaluation and she therefore had to answer a number of questions. First, how much would the evaluation cost? The costs included those incurred in collecting data on elderly needs and in compiling a record of current service provision – i.e. staff time, equipment, travel expenses, computer time, etc. This had to be considered in absolute terms but also in terms of the alternative purposes to which it could be put (for instance, increased service provision). Second, the manager had to estimate how much her staff who specialized in elderly work would resent and resist the evaluation. As part of this she had to examine whether other staff in the team serving other client groups would use this as an opportunity to pursue sectional interests. She also had to consider whether her senior management would listen constructively to the findings of the evaluation.

A third, broader area of the evaluation concerned those parties outside the service. Could she handle the criticisms which would arise if the study showed that the service was inadequate, particularly if this was due to a failure in the management of resources rather than in the expertise of specific workers? She had to balance possible future improvements in service against the possibility of being shown publicly that currently they were lacking. As in all service industries, the manager also had to consider her clients' reactions to the process. She had to guess how far the elderly in the area would seize upon this as an opportunity to voice their complaints (even if unfounded) and how far they would overestimate the latitude she had available for change, feeling very disappointed if any justifiable changes did not materialize. She considered how opposing political parties might use the findings in the media to their own ends.

Against these considerations she ranged her estimate of the potential improvements in services to the elderly that would be made if she could locate and remove practices or procedures which were wasteful or counter-productive. She thought about how her staff would react if they were found to be relatively successful. She estimated the boost in her team's reputation and the rhetorical mileage which could be made inside social services if she initiated this evaluation clearly signalling her intention to prove her team publicly accountable. Furthermore, she wondered whether the evaluation could help to set standards in services for the elderly in future. (It might then be used to assess her own bid to provide such services in the future against those of others once market testing had been introduced.)

In this case, the manager decided to go ahead with the evaluation. Not all factors had equal weight in her consideration. Although there were real penalties involved in the evaluation (primarily financial cost and staff anxiety), she anticipated major advantages for the client group and significant political and bureaucratic support for the decision.

It might be useful (see *Exercise* 2) to choose some aspect of the operation of the place where you work or where you have significant knowledge of the organization and assess whether an evaluation would pay off, even for something relatively minor. What becomes clear very quickly is that the ramifications of introducing an evaluation are diverse and wide-ranging. The 'ripple effect' as a consequence of evaluation is very marked and this phenomenon will be examined in a number of different contexts throughout the book.

The range of costs and benefits will depend to a large extent upon the model of evaluation that you use. The internal/invited/participatory type may be expected to evoke lower costs associated with resistance and anxiety, and greater benefits in terms of the feasibility of change following the evaluation. The external/imposed/non-participatory evaluation may be costly in anxiety, unwelcome results and ammunition for enemies, but totally satisfactory in providing innovatory and realistic suggestions for efficiency gains. Again, the major message here is that you need to mix and match, customizing the method to the problem you face: choose the model of evaluation which optimizes your gain. Evaluation can always pay off if you choose an appropriate time to do it, with correct targets and an objective which you understand well.

AN INITIAL EVALUATION ASSESSMENT

EXERCISE 2

Choose some aspect of the operation of the place where you work (or where you have significant knowledge of the organization) and assess whether a projected evaluation would pay off. It is sometimes interesting to do this cost – benefit analysis for an evaluation of a seemingly trivial activity of a large organization (for example, how the tea/coffee is provided). You should consider each of these aspects in turn:

- area of work
- your objectives and targets
- costs and benefits – e.g. financial outlay, anxiety caused, quality of improvements, etc.
- timing required

and assess the influence of these factors on your project:

- internal/external evaluation
- invited/imposed evaluation
- participatory/non-participatory evaluation

i.e. the eight models outlined on page 6.

Chapter Two

When To Evaluate

WHEN SHOULD YOU DO AN EVALUATION?

Sometimes you will have no choice about conducting an evaluation at a particular time because you are required by someone else to do so. This chapter does not deal with such occasions; rather, it deals with situations when the decision about when to evaluate can be influenced, or even determined, by you. It describes the major factors which should be taken into account in deciding when to schedule an evaluation.

In choosing when to start an evaluation three golden rules should be followed:

1. *Do not start an evaluation until you have specified at least one question which stands a good chance of being answered.* This rule could be formulated in the more robust form: do not start until you have a question which can be answered. It is not phrased in this way because there will be times when a question is important and clearly articulated but you feel uncertain whether the evaluation will yield sufficient information to answer it. The evaluation should not be pursued until the odds are in favour of you getting the answers that you need.

Having to be able to specify a potentially answerable question narrows the range of possible targets for, and scale of, the evaluation. Of course, it could be argued that all questions are answerable, given enough determination and resources. In reality, both are limited. For instance, ideally you may wish to evaluate the impact of some new operational philosophy upon the work and ethos of your entire organization. Realistically, though an evaluation might be designed which could yield an answer to this broad question, the costs of getting this answer would be so great that they would prohibit the work ever being done. Drawing up an answerable question is a fundamental part of designing an evaluation. The major advantage of employing outside experts is that they will be able to help you form your answerable question properly. The responsibility then lies with you to ensure that the question that they ultimately try to answer is really one you want answered. Sadly, the answerable questions are not always the interesting ones.

2. *Do not do an evaluation until you are sure that the answers it may provide have some chance of having an effect.* Evaluation has become a buzz word over recent years. It has connotations of management efficiency and responsiveness to clients, customers or funding agencies. To evaluate, and to be seen to evaluate, has become an end in itself. Public relations and image building is undoubtedly one justifiable reason for conducting evaluations. In such cases, whether the question is answered or not becomes a trivial consideration. What matters is simply the fact that the evaluation took place. Where evaluations are conducted with this public relations motive, the timing of the evaluation will be dictated by publicity schedules rather than by the prospect of its results having an effect.

Where the publicity hype is less significant the timing of an evaluation will depend more upon whether it stands a decent chance of producing any answers that will be taken seriously or have an effect. The result does not necessarily have to involve change; it can entail warding off prospective changes or simply offering an assurance that one needs to consider change. Whatever its recommendations, the evaluation should be timed to optimize the chance of it being given a fair hearing. There is no point in starting an evaluation when you (or other decision-makers) have no intention of acting upon it – unless it is conceived from inception as a public relations exercise.

3. *Do not begin an evaluation until you are satisfied that its benefits will outweigh its costs.* Much was said in Chapter 1 about calculating the costs and benefits of evaluation in the context of deciding whether to do one at all. The projection of costs and benefits may vary over time. In particular, cost factors may change and you may even decide to postpone an evaluation while you introduce some measures to reduce these costs. For instance, if staff resistance is expected to be a major cost you may be willing to plan a campaign to reduce resistance. The timing of the evaluation

would then depend upon your assessment that the balance of costs and benefits had been appropriately adjusted.

POINTLESS EVALUATION: INFORMATION, NOT INTELLIGENCE

There is a growing consensus in military circles that too often information is mistaken for intelligence. Electronic data-gathering technologies are now so advanced that military decision-makers can find themselves faced with too much information; more than they know what to do with. To be useful, information must not only be relevant but also structured. Transforming information into intelligence is first a process of imposing a structure upon it or, sometimes, identifying its intrinsic structure. *Structuring* is in turn primarily an issue of *filtering* the important bits from the rest, and of *linkage* – i.e. showing connections and hierarchies. The second process which translates information into intelligence entails *patterning* – i.e. identifying sequences of changes – and *recognition*, which involves noting the implications of changes.

Evaluations which provide information rather than intelligence can become pointless; they should only be started when the mechanism to translate the information into intelligence has been put in place. This essentially means knowing how you intend to use the data collected. If you have asked a precise and answerable question, coincidentally along the way you will have made many decisions about how you will use the data. The formulation of a precise question focuses the mind upon generating only useful data. The process of distilling the question requires that you address what information you really want and what you can do without.

Knowing how you want to use the data means more than just knowing what question you want answered. It also means knowing how you intend to analyse the data. Some of the statistical analyses that are often used in evaluation studies are described in other chapters, but here the point is different. Right from the beginning, you need to know how you intend to make sense of the information the evaluation generates. This orientation will dictate what techniques you use to describe the information, both qualitatively and quantitatively. The type of description adopted will later limit the *inferences* (that is, the meanings) which can be drawn from the information. This is why it is important to know at least in outline the structure you wish to use in translating the information gathered into intelligence before you start.

In order to understand a little more about the problems of posing answerable questions and translating information into intelligence, you might like to work through Exercise 3. Think through the problem and decide how you would tackle it before reading the section on what you should and shouldn't do. The secret to producing answerable questions and collecting usable information is specificity. The more specific you can be, the greater your chances of success.

POSING ANSWERABLE QUESTIONS

EXERCISE 3

If you were asked by a government to determine the impact of its health education upon tobacco use, what answerable question would you set for the evaluation study?

Write down the factors which you take into consideration when formulating the question. Indicate the sorts of conclusions which you could expect to draw from the information you collected in order to address the question.

Shoulds and Shouldn'ts
Read these only after trying the exercise. They represent just a few of the things you should have considered.

1. *You should have defined what health education you would be considering.*
Did you include all health education promulgated by the government in any shape or form? If so, you have a virtually unanswerable question, for budgetary, if for no other, reason. You need to be more precise, at least by separating health education which occurs in schools, in medical settings, in limited circulation media, and in mass advertising.

2. *You should have defined what types of impact on tobacco use you would be considering.*
Impact on tobacco use is too vague to be answerable in practice. You would need to specify at least the form of use: pipe, cigar, cigarette (filter/non-filter), and perhaps even chewing. You should have specified frequency and volume of use allowing for the possibility that health education has been known to backfire, increasing the behaviour targeted for reduction.

— *continued*

— continued —

3. *You should have defined over what period you would assess the impact.*
Would you be assessing the impact over a specific period of time? Would that be retrospectively or prospectively? Without a clear time-frame, the question inevitably would be unanswerable.

4. *You should have defined what sorts of people would be targeted in the exploration of the impact.*
Questions which entail assessing the impact of government health education upon everybody are practically unanswerable. Your question should indicate the part of the population that you would examine.

Being specific on these four issues will make it possible for you to anticipate better the types of inferences you would be able to draw from the data collected. If you were having difficulties in predicting what conclusions you could draw from the answer to your question, try working through it again, increasing its specificity.

EVALUATION BEFORE THE EVENT

Ideally, the best time to do an evaluation of some provision, practice or procedure would be before it was used. That way, if it turned out to be seriously flawed, corrections could be made before the problem started to become a handicap. Such anticipatory evaluations are actually possible and are done in a number of ways, with the two principal techniques of *simulation* and *meta-analysis*.

THE USE OF SIMULATION IN EVALUATION

Simulation revolves around being able to identify what variables (i.e. some measurable phenomena) you are interested in and how they relate to each other. The model of their relationships is often represented in terms of mathematical equations. Simulation techniques rely on being able to describe the parameters of the process you wish to evaluate with some degree of specificity. They allow you to manipulate the relationships between variables in the simulation model that you create so as to permit a range of possible 'futures' to be generated. Most simulation techniques involve computer models of the process. For example, if you wanted to know the likely impact of some advertising campaign upon the take-up of breast screening services in a locality it might be possible to model potential effects if you had data on the effects of other campaigns in similar communities. A computer simulation would allow you to base extrapolations upon existing data. In such a computer model it is possible to test the possible outcomes of different types of campaign by varying discrete aspects of the campaign separately.

In this world of simulated reality it is possible to explore the potential impacts of numerous variants of the target for evaluation. You can introduce small modifications to the representations of the process you wish to evaluate and monitor the effects on the overall operation of the model. In order to produce a useful simulation model you have to be able to do the things listed in the simulation checklist below. The process is complex and the novice might benefit from the help of an evaluation expert, at least on the first occasion that simulation is attempted.

THE SIMULATION CHECKLIST

In order to create a useful simulation model you need to be able to:

- identify all the variables relevant to the model
- represent the key characteristics of all variables in the model
- represent the relationships between all variables in the model
- represent the ways in which relationships between the variables change
- estimate the margin for error in the specification of these relationships.

NOTE: Representations of relationships are usually mathematical i.e. structural equations are used. Where an error margin cannot be specified some random factor is usually included to act as a cypher for it.

While simulation techniques tend to be regarded currently as feasible only for rich corporations and government departments, the rapidly widening availability of sophisticated computing software and hardware means that simulation evaluation will soon be within the grasp of most organizations. Of course, such simulations feed off data provided by earlier evaluations of allied or similar targets. To be any good, the simulation model needs good basic data. One of the implications of this is that if you want to use simulation (and the economies of speed it implies) in the future, you should probably be building a good database now so that it can be used later on.

Computer simulation in this sense is quite different from working through the evaluation in, for example, a role play or mock-up of the real situation. Simulation evaluation can also be conducted in such artificially created environments but the problems in drawing inferences from them are rather daunting. The effect of the unreality upon the phenomena to be investigated is usually quite literally unmeasurable – until, that is, you conduct the evaluation again outside of the role play in the natural environment and compare findings. Simulation in this instance merely provides indications of likely effects. Even so, simulations (or 'dummy runs' as they were called so graphically in the past) have a part in the evaluation process, particularly where complex, costly systems must be tested. The simulation in artificially created settings allows discrete aspects of the system to be evaluated separately. It allows for various combinations of system parts to be tested and new ways of linking them to be tried out systematically.

The simulation approach to evaluation is often linked with training. Simulations are used not only to assess the participants but also explicitly to train them. This confounding of assessment and training is usually regrettable, leading to a confusion of the two potential objectives of simulation and thus to neither being satisfied completely. In such simulations participants are never quite sure whether they should be showing that they can already do something or showing that they recognize the need to learn it. A good example of this problem comes from disaster exercises where the police, social services and health services simulate how they would handle a major accident (e.g. an aircraft crash) in order to assess the efficacy of their procedures.

Such exercises are meant to pinpoint weaknesses in the planned response. Often participants react to the exercise as if it was targeted at evaluating their personal skills and capacity to enact the plan. When aspects of the plan are weak, they are sometimes unwilling to reveal failures because they see this as reflecting badly upon themselves.

THE USE OF META-ANALYSES IN EVALUATION

Meta-analysis involves the statistical analysis of results from a large number of previous individual evaluation studies of the same or similar targets to distil general conclusions from their findings. It is, in fact, a way of systematically using such earlier studies to come to more generalizable and supportable conclusions. Meta-analysis is considered better than any straightforward review of the literature available on the topic because such reviews are rarely comprehensive, they underestimate the effects of methodological limitations on conclusions which can be drawn from studies, and they have difficulties in reconciling conflicting results from different data sets.

Meta-analysis uses a variety of statistical techniques which culminate in a summation of evaluation findings weighted to take into account the errors in sampling and measurement which characterized the original studies from which data were derived. As long as the thing which you propose to evaluate (or something very similar to it) has been the subject of prior evaluation, a meta-analysis will give you a valuable insight into what effects the thing is likely to have.

There are, however, obstacles to conducting a meta-analysis. First, you have to find previous studies which address the right target and which are concerned with assessing similar outcomes. For example, a museum curator may find many evaluations of museum displays available but it is questionable whether they will be relevant if the curator is only interested in one specific problem. This could be to measure, say, the impact of dinosaur exhibits upon 7 to 10-year-olds and their willingness to seek a career in science as a result of a museum visit. Second, you have to identify studies which used a similar means of measurement so as to allow genuine comparison of findings. For instance, to continue the example, even if all the evaluations of the museum displays actually were concerned with the impact on aspirations for a scientific career, they still may have measured aspirations in different ways. The question is: how to compare the extent of a given type of museum display's impact across studies? Typically, meta-analysis requires that the original studies provide data which will allow you to calculate an 'effect size'. The effect size basically reflects the absolute estimate of the average impact of the target for evaluation but modified to take account of the errors in sampling or measurement. In the example above an effect size might be calculated by looking at the average level of willingness to go into a science career amongst a class of school children who had been to a dinosaur exhibit and subtracting from it the average willingness to take up a science career among a class who had not visited the exhibit but were similar in all other respects, and dividing this by the amount of variation in the second group. The calculations of an effect size can be represented in an equation:

$$\frac{\text{Group 1 Mean Score on X} - \text{Group 2 Mean Score on X}}{\text{Standard Error of Mean of Group 2 on X}}$$

(where X is some feature of the group). Such effect sizes can be calculated for all the relevant studies, aggregated and their statistical significance can be calculated (see Chapter 5).

Meta-analysis is a valuable tool as a preliminary to your evaluation. References to comprehensive guides to meta-analysis are given under Further Reading at the end of the book. The major advantage that it has over rival methods is that it is relatively cheap and speedy. It may be considered an appropriate preliminary to any evaluation involving the collection of new data which can be costly. Of course, it will not give you an actual assessment of the impact of your target. Wherever possible a preliminary meta-analysis is advisable. You can avoid many problems in executing an evaluation based on new data when you start with a meta-analysis. As in all other ventures, in evaluation it is wise to learn from the experience of others.

EVALUATING PROCESS OR OUTCOME

To some extent the decision about when to evaluate will be dictated by whether you are assessing process or outcome. Process is the dynamic relationship between actions, resources and organizational structures which produces the effect. Outcome is the effect produced. Some evaluations will be concerned only with the effect, while others will be concerned only with how the effect is achieved. Some will be concerned with both the effect and its means of production. Inevitably, evaluations which are concerned with process need to start earlier than those focusing solely upon outcome.

Sometimes, this distinction between process and outcome is difficult to make. What is at one point the outcome of a process, later may become an intrinsic part of that process. The distinction relies on the time-scale applied. For instance, a company may introduce an innovative programme of induction for new staff which involves existing staff describing their early experiences in the job. The company may be interested in assessing the outcome in terms of the speed with which new employees reach some criterion productivity level. As these new employees become established, they in turn participate as trainers in the induction programme. Their early experiences of the job are, however, shaped by their own passage through the induction process. The process becomes reshaped by its own earlier outcomes. These feedback loops between outcome and process are common. The evaluator must therefore be willing to impose an arbitrary time-scale which defines what will be regarded as the process and what as the outcome.

EVALUATING COMPLEX, LONG-TERM OR DIFFUSE OUTCOMES

The evaluation of single, immediate, discrete outcomes can be relatively robust. If you want to know whether a worker is less likely to take time off work with back trouble in the month after her office is fitted with new chairs, an evaluation will give you the answer. Or if you need to know whether children attending one geography teacher's class are more likely to pass their end of term examinations than those in some other geography teacher's class, an evaluation will tell you. If you want to find out whether the elderly people attending a new community centre project are happier with it than its predecessor, an evaluation will show you. However, you may well be interested in outcomes which are multifaceted, drawn out over a long time, or distributed across different people and environments. Evaluation of complex, long-term or diffuse outcomes itself becomes complex, long-term and diffuse and should be embarked upon only after careful thought and planning.

Of course, some of the most important outcomes that you need to evaluate are complex, long-term or diffuse but the need to evaluate such outcomes cannot be ignored. The very purpose of your organization or your activity may well be to produce such outcomes. You may feel that evaluating anything less would not assess the real impact of your efforts.

Cultural and leisure enterprises are particularly prone to this sort of problem. For example, the director of a museum who is planning the opening of a new gallery may believe that the true impact of the gallery needs to be assessed in terms of its effects upon the aesthetic life of the community. The director may be concerned with outcome in terms of the general appreciation of artistic endeavour, artistic literacy, and, within that, in terms of the emotional reaction to the works within the museum. These outcomes, which the director believes justify the very existence of the new gallery, are complex, long-term and diffuse. In one sense, the problem arises because the outcomes are 'invisible'. Emotional and aesthetic reactions (the 'feel good' factor) are not easy to objectify. In another sense, the problem arises because the outcomes are spread across many individuals who together comprise the community on which the impact of the gallery must be assessed. In yet another sense, the problem arises because the effect of the gallery may not be direct. It may change a community, not because people are exposed to it directly but because they are exposed to people who have been exposed to it. In other words, the gallery may have its effect

---

THE MUSEUM DIRECTOR'S PROBLEM

The museum director could evaluate the following sub-outcomes. All can be said to contribute to an understanding of the impact of the new gallery upon the aesthetic life of the community:

- Changes in attendance levels at the museum after the opening of the new gallery.
- Changes in attendance at other artistic venues or events post-opening.
- Changes in financial support for artistic endeavours provided by members of the community.
- Changes in uptake of arts education locally.
- Emotional reactions and attitudes of visitors after seeing the gallery.
- Amount of local discussion of the gallery (by individuals and the media).
- Changes in knowledge about the art forms represented in the gallery in visitors and the community more generally.

NOTE: Of course, in each case the design of the evaluation would need to ensure that if changes were monitored in these potential outcomes, they were attributable to the opening of the new gallery and not to some other factor.

---

through a form of 'contagion'. This would then become an example of the problem discussed earlier where initial outcome becomes part of the process.

The only viable solution to the problems of evaluating complex, long-term and diffuse outcomes is to break them down into their constituent elements. The task of the evaluator is to carve these 'big' outcomes into bite-sized chunks. You might try, for example, as an exercise to list the elements which the director of the museum should take into account when assessing the impact of a new gallery upon the aesthetic life of the community. In doing this it would be valuable to consider how each outcome could be indexed (that is, described or measured). Some of the sub-outcomes that could be examined are summarized in the box opposite. If you have done this assessment, you will have realized that it is a process of unpicking the global question into its constituent parts in order to produce answerable questions.

BUILDING EVALUATION INTO THE INITIAL DESIGN OF TARGETS

So far the discussion has treated the process of evaluation as something which is separate from its targets. At some level they will always be distinct but in practice the machinery of evaluation may be incorporated into the target it assesses. Evaluation is increasingly designed into the structure of provisions, practices and procedures. What this means is that, for instance, in the case of a provision such as a building, it will be structurally designed to operate instruments which measure the parameters of functions which need to be evaluated (e.g. computer systems are included which monitor temperature and energy usage). In the case of operational procedures which are being evaluated, part of the procedure itself will be to collect data for the evaluation. These built-in evaluations can be designed to provide continuous on-line information or 'intermittent sampling'. They are probably the very best way to evaluate process.

MANAGEMENT INFORMATION SYSTEMS (MIS)
Archetypical examples of the mechanisms of in-built evaluations come from some new management information systems, computer programs which allow you to monitor the operation of many aspects of a complex organization (as long as those aspects are recorded on or operated through networked computers). Evaluation then becomes an intrinsic and non-intrusive part of the

operation of the organization. This shift to being non-intrusive (at least at the point of data gathering) is valuable since some of the more obvious costs of evaluation associated with resistance and anxiety are removed. Obviously, to be any good, any given management information system must receive accurate information appropriate for the evaluation undertaken.

There is still scepticism in some quarters about the usefulness of management information systems. Like all data-gathering techniques, the practice can be subverted wilfully as well as accidentally. In using these systems for evaluation, it is essential that you ensure that they are secure against interference. It is also vital that you actually understand the basis for the data generated because the systems can flood you with information. The safeguards described earlier need to be applied so that it is intelligence rather than information which is produced.

Built-in evaluations usually result in on-going or intermittent feedback which is allowed to alter the process monitored. This reinforces the fact that the evaluation is no longer separate from the process it assesses. It also has the effect of making evaluation normative: i.e. something to be expected and accepted. Along the way, it often educates those involved about evaluation methods and reduces the likelihood that they will be duped by false conclusions from an evaluation or misled by poor data. Built-in evaluations have the major advantage that they are so much a part of the process that the changes they suggest are less likely to be resisted.

Given that the focus of this chapter is on when to evaluate, it should be added that built-in evaluations can be introduced at any point. They do not have to be in place at the very start, though this is useful; they can be introduced later. Built-in evaluation has one further advantage. Because it absorbs evaluation into the process, the apparent costs of conducting the evaluation can be absorbed into operational costs. Of course, the merits of this will depend on whether you are responsible for an evaluation budget or an operational budget.

THE ETHICS OF EVALUATION

Whenever you conduct an evaluation you face myriad ethical questions; these also will have an impact upon when it is appropriate to do an evaluation. Some of the main ethical issues are listed in the box.

ETHICAL ISSUES IN EVALUATION

- Who should be told that the evaluation is occurring?

- If people are involved in the evaluation should they be told that it is happening? Should they be told about its purpose?

- Is it justifiable to mislead informants about the purpose of the evaluation in order to be able to collect more reliable and valid data?

- Should permission be acquired from the individuals concerned before data on them is collected? (This is distinct from simply informing them that you will be collecting data.)

- Who should be told about the results of the evaluation?

- How far should data, as distinct from conclusions, be made public?

- Should conclusions be open to verification by interested parties or individuals?

- Who owns the data? Who can use it?

The purpose of this section is to alert you to the ethical issues, but not to suggest that there are right and wrong answers to each of the questions posed. Ethical issues rarely allow absolute solutions. In thinking about evaluations that you have been involved with or which you anticipate conducting, you may find that there are other ethical questions which arise. Anyone doing an evaluation must be sensitive to these issues.

Before doing an evaluation you must have at least a provisional answer to each of the issues posed in the box. Answers might be provisional because you may feel that before committing yourself you need to see what the data reveal; for example, on the question of whether the data will be made public. This may be sensible but there is a problem in making answers to these ethical questions too conditional on what turns up. If you are uncertain, people are more likely to be able to manipulate you to satisfy their objectives. For example, if you do not say categorically that data will not be made public you may find that your intentions are assumed by other people. Some may assume you will go public; others will assume that you will not. Both sides will react to the evaluation in terms of their assumptions about your intentions. This may be just what you want but it can get out of hand if, for instance, some people try to use the fact that you did not correct any misunderstanding they might have had of your intentions as a lever to make you act in the way they expected you would. This probably seems rather convoluted but anyone who has conducted an evaluation will recognize that the parties involved use many types of argument. Manipulating the perceived ethical quality and standing of the evaluation is a central tactic. As the evaluator, it is useful to ensure such manipulation is eliminated by clarifying your own ethical position right from the outset. At the very least, by the start of the evaluation you have to know what stance you will take on privacy and disclosure. This will directly influence your data collection design. Consequently, a fourth golden rule can be added to the three with which this chapter started: *do not begin an evaluation until you are satisfied that you appreciate fully all the ethical implications.*

Chapter Three

Mapping the Strategy: Designing an Evaluation

In this chapter we consider how various strategies of evaluation can be reconciled with the difficulties of working in the real world. Traditionally, strategies of evaluation have been bound by the rigorous demands of the experimental method. Whilst the technical validity of the findings is important, it is difficult to envisage being able to capture the subtleties and complexities of real-life phenomena in a truly experimental way. This chapter illustrates how some of the practical difficulties of evaluation can be solved, minimized and avoided in your choice of design strategy.

Although interrelated, a distinction between 'design' and 'measurement' issues can be made in evaluation work. Design refers to the strategy or schedule used to collect the evidence you require, to analyse the findings and draw conclusions. Measurement is concerned with systematizing the information which is collected and standardizing its unit of recording. This chapter focuses on design (i.e. mapping the strategy of the evaluation exercise), while measurement issues are dealt with in subsequent chapters.

STEPS IN DESIGNING AN EVALUATION

The checklist overpage identifies the main steps in designing an evaluation.

Most central to considerations of design is the need to be conversant with a range of different design types and how best to use them. You will need to note that each design presupposes that something has occurred or is occurring which needs to be

---

STEPS IN DESIGNING AN EVALUATION

Specify the event to be evaluated
* Define the broad issues.
* Set priorities against strategic goals, time and resources.
* Seek agreement on the nature and scope of the task.

Specify the form of the impact and on whom
* Identify the information/evidence required and from whom.
* Identify intended outcomes in tangible terms.
* Define the criteria of success, i.e. how will you know that the outcome has been successfully reached?

Determine the time-frame

Design the Evaluation
* Create alternative options for achieving specified outcomes.
* Identify obstacles/constraints associated with each option and weed out unworkable solutions.
* Identify the most feasible option given the circumstances.

Specify the measures of impact
* Identify and select methods of gathering information/evidence.
* Identify and select appropriate forms of measurement.

Determine who collects the data and the deadline

---

evaluated in terms of its outcomes. Here this occurrence is referred to as an 'event' meaning the activity (i.e. the practice or procedure) under scrutiny. The event may be either an everyday occurrence or something which is staged specifically for evaluation purposes. The latter usually involves an 'intervention' of some kind – e.g. staff go on a training course, or a new practice or procedure is introduced. The evaluation of an intervention follows the same logic as the drug trial: something new is tried out and its outcomes are then compared in some way to the old way of doing things to see whether any improvement has been made.

You will also need to note how the designs vary in the degree of control the evaluator is able to exert over the target event (i.e. the character of the event and the logistics of its implementation).

The 'Now' Design below, for example, assumes little if any control of the target event by the evaluator whereas the 'Before-and-after Design with Controls' requires that he or she exert quite strict control over what happens, with whom, exactly how and when.

TYPES OF DESIGN

THE 'NOW' DESIGN

Event ⟶ description and/or measurement

This is the simplest of all designs. It involves a description of an ongoing event (such as an operating procedure or shiftwork pattern) in relation to a particular outcome of interest (for example, work efficiency and effectiveness) over a fixed time. Typically, the event to be described will be the province of a specific group of people whose working circumstances are of interest. The advantages of the Now Design:

1. It enables a more in-depth examination of a particular situation than other designs.
2. The information it yields can be rich and enlightening, and may provide new leads or raise questions that otherwise might never have been asked.
3. The people involved usually comprise a fairly well circumscribed and captive group making it possible for the evaluator to describe the attitudes or behaviour of most if not all of them.
4. Information about processes can be derived.

Problems with the Now Design arise largely from difficulties with interpretation. There is really no way of being able to determine the impact of an event that has not been systematically controlled or where there is an absence of baseline information against which impacts can be compared.

One way of overcoming the difficulty of interpretation is to compare the outcomes to some **absolute standard** of success (i.e. something agreed in advance as the criterion against which the event – usually performance – can be compared). These standards are now set at an international level: for example, the BS ENISO 9000 (formerly BS5750) provides criteria for judging the quality of a product, a process or performance in British industry; and the national standards of educational attainment provide developmental milestones or 'norms' against which the performance of schoolchildren can be evaluated. The practices of any one particular organization can therefore be evaluated against the BS ENISO 9000 criteria: if it achieves the standards represented by these criteria then it can be granted BSI approval. Otherwise the need for change in specific areas is highlighted. Similarly, the performance of teachers may be evaluated against the national standards. If they do not live up to these, then the criteria can be used as a framework to pin-point any aspects of change required. Other standards are defined and agreed at a more local level: for example, company or departmental standards embodied in the 'business plan', or personnel policy regarding the practice of equal opportunities. Whilst the above shows how the problem of interpretability can be overcome there are other weaknesses associated with the Now Design. These include:

1. Getting too close to the minutiae of things, which can make it difficult to 'see the wood for the trees'.
2. Getting so involved that impartiality is lost.
3. The information yielded by the Now Design can be difficult and time-consuming to quantify and analyse.
4. The Now Design yields evidence with implications that cannot be generalized beyond local circumstances.
5. The people involved may feel under intense scrutiny, apprehensive about being 'evaluated' and/or resentful because they fear for their jobs.

THE 'BEFORE-AND-AFTER' DESIGN

Test 1 ⟶ event ⟶ Test 2

This design is more systematic than the Now Design. It involves assessing the impact of an event on something by comparing outcomes before and after the occurrence of a particular event. The information obtained before the event provides the kind of baseline information that is otherwise absent from the Now Design against which to monitor and judge the significance of any change. By comparing pre-event with post-event information, evidence for gains or losses occurring can be derived which can be matched against those expected. The group involved may be a natural one (e.g. a specific group of managers) or may be formed for the purpose (e.g. a sample of managers from across the organization). An example of this might be where managers' communication skills are assessed before and after being involved in a 'Management Development Workshop'. This design is possible only if:

1. You have the opportunity to take a measurement before the commencement of the event being examined.
2. It is meaningful to take a measurement in advance of the event; it would be futile to measure something not yet acquired.
3. The measurement tool will not induce certain trains of thought and feeling that can bias the way the individual responds to the event (e.g. defensiveness).
4. It is possible to use the same measurement tool before and after the event. If there are changes of instrumentation then the information yielded will not be comparable.
5. It is feasible in terms of the resources available.

Even given the advantages of the Before-and-after Design, there is still no guarantee that the event can be assumed to be the true explanation for the observed outcome. Alternative interpretations are possible. For example, it may be that between pre-event testing and post-event testing a lot of people dropped out of the study in which case the composition of the sample may differ. Another explanation could be that the participants simply matured over the course of the intervention and would have improved anyway. This might occur, for example, where managers feel under pressure to adopt a different way of communicating with subordinates, anyway, because of organizational imperatives.

Detailing (as in the natural group) or controlling (as in the constructed group) the composition of the sample is important for the interpretation of the findings. For instance, the managers may be of mixed ability (i.e. some very good, some very poor, some okay) or of comparable ability (i.e. all very poor communicators). In the case of the mixed ability group the outcome of an event designed to improve communication skills will be less easily interpreted than in the case of managers whose skills are initially comparable especially if they are all considered 'poor' (hence the need for a training event). Since the latter is an extreme group, then the ability measure taken after the event will inevitably yield higher scores than those obtained at pre-event testing purely through chance. Consequently, the origins of any improvement that does occur cannot be automatically ascribed to the event.

The above problems can to some extent be eased if contextual information is also obtained throughout the duration of the event. This will necessitate gathering information about the process and

THE TIME-SERIES 'BEFORE-AND-AFTER' DESIGN VARIATION

Some of the problems of interpretation and bias associated with the Before-and-after Design can be overcome with a Time-series approach. This involves taking measurements from a group of people on an intermittent basis both before and after the event of interest as illustrated below.

Test 1 → Test 2 → Test 3 → event → Test 4 → Test 5 → Test 6

In this way, an answer to the question 'Does the event of interest disturb the trend in the occurrence of things?' is provided. For example, if an improvement is made from Test 1 to Test 2 in the ordinary Before-and-after Design there is no way of telling whether it would have been made anyway.

Take the following example: Care workers in a residential care unit participate in a 'control and restraint' workshop designed to improve their ability to handle instances of child violence. To rule out the influence of experience in handling child violence as opposed to the intervention in producing improvement the evaluation would need to show that there was no systematic trend of improvement before the event (e.g. nine, six, and three months before) and which was maintained after the event (e.g. three, six and nine months after). The event should produce a sudden improvement in behaviour (i.e. it disrupts the trend) for it to be deemed a success over and above everyday experience. Regular post-intervention measurement also enables the evaluator to determine the power of an intervention to produce lasting effects.

The Time-series Design is costly in terms of resources and might also be experienced as very intrusive because of the need for repeated measurement. Moreover, repeated measurement can itself engender change because of the 'rehearsal' of certain of the skills and abilities entailed. These disadvantages can be outweighed if:

1. The measurement process can be timetabled into the regular course of events as in the above example.

— continued —

continued —

2. It is not feasible to employ a comparison group against which to assess the impact of the intervention.
3. It is of interest to monitor the impact of certain events on a long-term basis by ruling out the influence of other factors on the outcomes obtained.
4. The 'rehearsal effect' is accounted for or controlled out at the analysis stage. Measures of behaviour that occur in the natural course of things are less likely to be 'contaminated' by the opportunity for rehearsal.

circumstances of the event such as who and what kind of activities are involved, what materials were used and when, what else happened during the process, who dropped out and why, whether there were any problems or difficulties that arose, and so on. This information can be used to help make sense of the findings obtained using the Before-and-after Design. It is important to gather this kind of information about what is actually happening at the time rather than in retrospect, though interviewing participants after the event in order to seek explanations for the findings obtained is better than nothing. In Chapter 5 we show how this kind of contextual information can be built into the analysis process, for example in investigating the relative power of particular factors to predict a given outcome.

'BEFORE-AND-AFTER' DESIGN WITH CONTROLS

Treatment group	Test 1 ⟶ event ⟶ Test 2	
Comparison group	Test 1 ⟶ no (or alternative) event ⟶ Test 2	

This design is a quasi-experimental adaptation of the conventional control group design where samples are randomly obtained and assigned to 'conditions'. In the conventional design random assignment means that groups are equivalent insofar as a non-biased distribution of the various characteristics that might systematically influence the outcome (i.e. which otherwise may not have been considered) is assured. However, randomization is rarely feasible in practice. In the adapted design, the groups are assembled beforehand to be as similar as availability permits. The practical advantage of this design is that intact groups can be employed; minimal disruption is caused since the evaluation is embedded as far as possible into the natural course of events.

Examples of this design are numerous. For instance with one of two groups of care workers equivalent in all respects before any intervention they receive – i.e. they do the same type of work, have similar socio-economic status, educational ability and gender composition. The intervention in this case is a workshop designed to help care workers handle HIV/AIDS patients and their relatives. Both groups are, however, required to complete an inventory of attitudes and behaviour towards HIV/AIDS patients and their relatives three months in advance of the workshop (where neither group is informed about the workshop scheduled). Three months after the workshop, care workers from both groups complete the inventory of attitudes and behaviours again. It is expected that care workers involved in the workshop would express more positive and less discriminatory attitudes towards patients with HIV/AIDS afterwards and would be more likely to deal with the patients and their relatives in an informed, compassionate and constructive manner than (a) before, and (b), than care workers who were not involved in the workshop.

Procedurally it is crucial to ensure that the groups are treated fairly much the same except for the intervention to which the 'treatment group' is exposed. If some difference between the results of the two groups is obtained after the intervention, a more powerful conclusion can be drawn about its influence (as long as the possibility of the groups being different anyway can be ruled out). Otherwise it could be said that there were more ways than one of accounting for the difference obtained. The credibility of the findings depends on the ability of the evaluator to demonstrate that the treatment and comparison are 'alike' except for the intervention received. In the above example, some indication of this would be given by the pattern of attitudes and behaviours demonstrated by both groups in advance of the workshop. If there are no substantial differences then one could argue that, for the purposes of the study, they were equivalent. Consequently, any differences obtained after the workshop can be more reliably attributed to the fact of the intervention. But trying to find out exactly how similar groups are is a difficult task because there are so many characteristics that can affect someone's reactions to an intervention. Again, with the example given, there could be many other factors at play which influence care workers' reactions to the HIV/AIDS workshop; for example, someone known personally to care workers may be diagnosed HIV positive, a media event may have occurred, and so on. Problems can occur with this design if:

1. The influence of the intervention strategy has effects which are 'leaked' to the comparison group.
2. Members of each group are aware that they are involved in an experiment of some kind which may bias their responses to the intervention.
3. The groups are treated differently in ways other than purely in terms of the intervention.

It is not feasible to use this design if:

1. Comparable groups are not available or cannot be constructed.
2. It is unethical to withhold treatment from one of the groups. This might be overcome by having the groups take it in turns to be the treatment group, where the comparison group is entered into the treatment after a short delay.
3. There are practical constraints on how much control can be exerted during the event (e.g. inability to exert total control over the way the two groups are treated, ensuring the intervention happens entirely according to plan).

THE 'NOW AND THEN' DESIGN VARIATION

In this design comparison groups are assumed to be equivalent (or at least comparable) at the start, hence the absence of the pre-test component. This is useful if there are no pre-tests available, if it is too inconvenient or costly to employ them or if they might bias the way that people respond to the intervention. It is also possible that asking people to complete the same test again could lead them into thinking that they are supposed to have changed their attitudes and behaviours in the time between Test 1 and Test 2 irrespective of whether or not they were involved in the intervention. In short, the Before-and-after Design contains subtle demands for change. This consideration must be weighed up against the risk associated with the assumption of 'equivalence' in the post-test only design.

Treatment group	Event ⟶	**Test 1**
Comparison group	No Event ⟶	**Test 2**

continued

continued —

This post-test only design is feasible if the issue of evaluation arises only once the intervention is under way. The usefulness of this design is also highlighted in instances where it would be nonsensical to employ a pre-test. An example is provided from probationary work by the issue of 'reoffending'. By definition this will occur after an intervention, in which case pre-testing is never an issue. The evaluator's task may be to document the frequency and nature of the reoffending behaviour of two or more samples of young offenders after receiving one of two or more types of intervention (e.g. probation with community service, or housing in an institution for young offenders). The different interventions are then compared to see which, if any, of the interventions is most successful at preventing reoffence.

The problem with this kind of study is that it is concerned mainly with 'outcomes' at the expense of 'process': the evaluator may or may not have control over, or even access to, the intervention programme. Consequently it would be difficult to identify what exactly it is about the intervention(s) that made it work (or otherwise). It may nonetheless provide some preliminary evidence for the relative preventative power of certain types of intervention and might even strengthen the case for a more sophisticated study.

OPTIMIZE THE DESIGN SOLUTION

Results from a rigorously conducted evaluation are hard to refute, even by sceptics. The degree of control built into the design is central to this, affecting the whole point of view about the seriousness of the enterprise and about how information will be gathered, analysed and presented. At the same time, the design solution will be compromised by practicalities such as:
– the **scale** of the event being evaluated
– the **level** at which the event is pitched
– who the **evaluator** is and how that person is perceived in relation to the event.

THE SCALE OF THE EVENT

The event may involve a well circumscribed group of people (e.g. all care workers in a particular institution) or a diffuse and heterogeneous category of people (e.g. all employees of an organization undergoing large-scale change). In the latter it would not be feasible to build much 'evaluative rigour' into the design solution whilst in the former a neater, more controlled design solution might be possible. Basically, a group can comprise anything from two people to two million people: group members may know each other but in many instances they will not.

THE LEVEL OF THE EVENT

The level at which the event is pitched is inextricably linked with the scale of the intervention. Using the care worker example, evaluation at the level of individual performance would be most appropriate e.g. how care workers respond to a particular training intervention. To evaluate the impact of organizational change, however, raises sampling issues: only a relatively small proportion of employees are likely to be involved in the evaluation exercise. One may narrow the target group down to involve a particular group of employees but this would still require consideration of the criteria for inclusion/exclusion and how to enlist their support. The following box outlines some of the available sampling strategies.

THE ISSUE OF SAMPLING

This addresses the question: 'Evidence about what and from whom?'. The answer might seem obvious. If, say, you need to find out how managers handle shortfalls in performance, obviously evidence is sought from the managers themselves. However, it is not as simple as this. Although in many evaluation exercises the definition of the people involved in the practices concerned is well circumscribed, in some instances it is not. Moreover, even if it is clearly defined it may not be feasible or necessary to involve everyone or to gather evidence from everyone which raises the question of what criteria of inclusion/exclusion to use. The difficulty is making sure that those you sample represent as far as possible the target population as a whole

─ *continued* ─

— *continued* —

(e.g. all managers/all managers working in a particular type of organization or all managers within one particular organization). This means that the evidence you acquire from the sample should, in principle, be the same kind of evidence you would acquire if you involved the larger group or the entire population of interest.

Representativeness can be ensured by randomly selecting people from the population of interest (e.g by drawing their names out of a hat). In practice a **random sample** is difficult to achieve. Circumstances can dictate the composition of the sample. There are also many instances where the group selected is prescribed by the event in question (e.g. all managers whose skills in handling performance shortfalls are suspect). This is known as '**pinpoint selection**' because the sample is a *purposive* one. In cases like this where the sample cannot be guaranteed to be representative of a larger group, strictly speaking the results of the evaluation cannot be generalized beyond that of the actual group involved.

Another type of non-random sampling applicable to evaluation work is known as **quota sampling**. This occurs in instances where you wish certain characteristics to be featured in your sample (e.g. equal number of males and females or people of a certain status or age).

Sampling issues are important since how you construct your sample will influence the type of conclusions that you draw from your findings and the relevance of the recommendations that you form from them.

THE EVALUATOR

When the evaluator is closely involved in whatever is under evaluation the task of assessing its impact has different implications than if they were able to take a completely distant and impartial view. In one instance they may become too close to the day-to-day minutiae of things whilst in the other they risk feeling alienated from the situation because of peoples' reactions to being evaluated from such an abstract standpoint. This also alludes to how the evaluator is perceived by others. For example, someone known to be very senior within an organization may bring about responses

STRATEGY AGAINST VARIATIONS BETWEEN
EVALUATOR AND EVALUATED

Internal evaluation
➤ Develop and maintain an impartial stance.
➤ Identify and test your assumptions by asking questions.
➤ Clarify the nature of your role, its power basis and range of responsibilities.
➤ Identify key audiences and their range of concerns.
➤ Clarify goals and objectives.
➤ Keep sight of the wider picture.

External evaluation
➤ Manage personal credibility and gain trust.
➤ Secure the co-operation of others.
➤ Secure local knowledge, facilities and resources.
➤ Identify who is 'who', their roles, responsibilities and power bases.
➤ Clarify organizational/departmental reporting and communication structures.
➤ Identify key audiences, their expectations and concerns.
➤ Secure agreement on the nature and scope of your task.

Imposed evaluation
➤ Identify sources of resentment, hostility and organizational inertia and develop strategies for managing them.
➤ Manage personal credibility and gain trust by acknowledging feelings and concerns.
➤ Develop and maintain an impartial stance.
➤ Secure access to information, check its validity and reliability.

Invited evaluation
➤ Identify the source of the invitation and the extent of consensus underpinning it.
➤ Clarify the range of expectations, feelings and concerns.
➤ Secure agreement on the nature of your task, your roles and responsibilities.
➤ Identify the uses to which the evaluation information will be put.
➤ Review the implications of positive and negative findings.

continued

— *continued* —

Participatory evaluation

➤ Identify key audiences and their expectations, needs and concerns.

➤ Minimize audience anxiety and gain their trust.

➤ Clarify the extent of agreement on the nature and scope of the evaluation exercise.

➤ Identify the evidence required and gain access to it.

➤ Secure the co-operation and commitment of those involved.

➤ Identify and characterize the range of constraints.

➤ Determine the extent of others' involvement in considerations of strategy and method.

➤ Check validity and reliability of information provided.

➤ Keep sight of the goals and objectives guiding the evaluation.

Non-Participatory evaluation

➤ Gain credibility and trust by demonstrating objectivity and evaluation expertise.

➤ Identify the nature, range and source of evidence required and secure access to it.

➤ Identify any legal or ethical constraints on access to information.

➤ Plan data handling and analysis at the outset.

that are completely the opposite to those engendered by someone more junior; examples could range from positivity and acquiescence to negativity and disillusionment, in extreme cases. Variations in the relationship between the evaluator and evaluated are described in the box above (page 43), using the various dimensions from Chapter 1. Awareness of these differences, and strategies to avoid their influence, can help in evaluation design.

Problems may also arise for those who have little control over the design of the evaluation, which can happen when evaluation is an afterthought conducted in retrospect. To help in handling this kind of situation the next section provides guidelines on the sorts of questions that will need to be asked.

EVALUATION IN RETROSPECT

When evaluation is conducted in retrospect you will need to ask detailed questions to ascertain the nature of the event under scrutiny and its context. The sort of questions which should be posed are presented in the checklist below:

- How was the event staged? Was it something which occurred in the normal run of things or was it implemented in a 'controlled' way? How was the event managed? (For example: how many 'treatments' were involved? Were control or comparison groups employed?)

- What were the characteristics of the control/comparison group relative to those of the 'treatment' groups?

- How were the 'groups' constructed (e.g. volunteers, a pre-assembled group, or one randomly selected)?

- What was the time-scale of the event (e.g. before-and-after, time-series)?

- Were any of the participants lost? If so why, and what were their characteristics (e.g. did they differ from those who stayed in the programme)?

- How suitable was the design for the issues being addressed and the outcomes being achieved?

- What evidence is there for *internal* validity of the design? (For example, is it possible to identify and minimize 'contaminants' or 'confounding factors' that may otherwise obscure the causal link between event and outcome?) What evidence is there for *external* validity of the design? (This might be generalizability or the extent to which the outcomes would be duplicated were the same event staged at a different place, time and with different participants.)

- Which group is the focus of the event and why? The impact of an event, no matter how well designed and implemented, might be nil if the target group is inappropriate or ill-specified.

- How sensitive were the criteria for inclusion/exclusion in the study? How thoroughly are sample characteristics identified and detailed?

In addition to obtaining information on inputs and activities, information will need to be sought on the broader aspects of managing the event and its social and political context. It is necessary to know whether the event went as planned and, if not, what the problems and difficulties were.

Evaluation is rarely cut and dried: an 'ideal' design may turn out to be impossible to implement because of the complex social, political and managerial milieu extant. There will be a constant tension between what constitutes a good design and what is practically possible. Some fundamental questions that need to be answered in the process of mapping evaluation strategy are listed in the following box.

QUESTIONS IN MAPPING EVALUATION STRATEGY

– What kind of evidence is required?
– For what purpose is the evidence required?
– Who wants the evidence and by when?
– Who else has a stake in the outcomes? What kind of stake is it?
– In what form should the evidence be?
– What design and measurement instruments will be accepted as yielding credible sources of evidence?
– What kind of resources are being committed to the evaluation?
– What kind of budgetary constraints are there?
– To what extent is the event to be evaluated already up and running?
– Who is involved in the event and in what capacity?
– What scope is there to plan from scratch?
– What exactly are the conditions and constraints around which evaluation strategy must be mapped?
– How realistic are the goals given the time-scale and resources?
– What exactly is your role in the event to be evaluated?
– What exactly is your role in the evaluation process?
– Is there any area of your involvement where you have absolute jurisdiction?
– Who is responsible for recording the impact of the event to be evaluated?
– What will happen to the findings? Who is responsible for interpreting the impact, forming and implementing any recommendations made?

Chapter Four

Evaluation Tactics: Collecting Data and Imposing Measurement

The choice of method for gathering information is part of the evaluation design: the method must suit the task. Methods can be used in combination; the weaknesses of one can be balanced by the strengths of another. This chapter provides guidelines for method selection, identifying the advantages and disadvantages of various types. A step-by-step guide to developing and using these methods is provided also, with examples.

EVIDENCE AND THE ISSUE OF MEASUREMENT

Measurement is about obtaining **evidence** for something and **quantifying** data in some manageable way (i.e. assigning numbers to it). To use the distinction made in Chapter 2, it entails translating information into intelligence. Some things are easier to measure than others. Behaviour is more accessible than knowledge, feelings or attitudes because, potentially, it can be observed. Evidence of what people know, how they feel and what they think about something must be derived in more indirect ways, for example, by asking questions or providing statements against which individuals can indicate their extent of agreement. For example: 'How do you feel about plans to introduce performance-related pay?' Response: 'It will increase employees' commitment to their jobs'. Two key questions are therefore:

- What is the nature of the evidence you require?
- How can you best secure this evidence?

TYPES OF METHOD

There are several methods of obtaining evidence of interest to the evaluator:

Asking questions	*Observing Behaviour*	*Existing sources*
Interviews	Observations	Secondary sources
Questionnaires (including tests and attitude scales)		

The main considerations guiding choice of method are listed in the box below. Much will depend on the willingness of people to co-operate with the project and to commit the necessary time and effort. The more time-consuming or intrusive the method the more difficult it is to secure the commitment required.

CRITERIA FOR SELECTING A METHOD

The problem or task

Project objectives
What type of information do I need?
• Procedures
• Behaviours
• Beliefs/Opinions
• Knowledge
• Abilities/Competences
• Attitudes

How can I get this type of information?

Sources of evidence

Ask questions   Observe behaviour   Existing records
– Who and how many people will be providing the relevant information?
– How many people will be helping me to gather the information?
– Are they appropriately trained?
– How much time have I/we got?
– What kinds of resources do I/we have?
– What are the advantages and disadvantages of each method relative to the task?

OBSERVATION

The observation procedure is as follows:

- ➤ 1. prepare a sampling plan
- ➤ 2. produce an observation schedule
- ➤ 3. select and train the observers
- ➤ 4. prepare the participants
- ➤ 5. conduct the observations
- ➤ 6. score, interpret and analyse the evidence.

Each of these steps is described below using a case example about performance-related pay in a factory. In this example, the task is to evaluate the work activities (i.e. conduct a series of 'job evaluations') of factory operators in a food processing plant using a Now Design. The organization has adopted a policy of biannual appraisal which requires that all employees work to agreed job descriptions against which their performance is assessed and their pay is related on a scale. To date, pay differentials have been produced by length of service. The intention is to change the system to one of performance-related pay. Since the original job descriptions have not been revised to account for changes in working practice introduced by automation, they need updating to make it possible to identify performance differentials. Specifically, the aim is to derive information on three job components:

– What does the operator do? (actions)
– Under what conditions does he/she perform these activities? (conditions)
– How well does the operator do it? (standards)

It will require that one or more observers devote their attention to the work activities of a sample of operators within their daily work setting (including night shifts) and for prescribed periods of time. You may be given precise guidelines of who and what to observe, when and how long to observe and the method of recording information by the project coordinators, or you may have to decide these things for yourself. The more formal and structured the observation process the more mechanized it will be. The observer(s) will need to be well rehearsed in the observation process. Where sensitivities are likely to be aroused a highly structured approach to observation is recommended. This will add credibility to the observation process since it will appear well planned and professional.

STEP 1: PREPARE A SAMPLING PLAN
It is rarely possible to observe everyone or everything. Candidates,
activities, events or procedures – whatever the focus of the observation, will need to be selected. Who or what you end up observing
may also depend on people's willingness to co-operate. In this
example, jobs are being observed. Three operators per job (across
eight different jobs) are selected by the Operations Manager as
'standard setters' (i.e. high, average, low). This kind of initial
categorization (based on shop floor knowledge) is an important
starting point for the identification of more fine-grained job differentials. Shift managers – whose help is enlisted – confirm that
these initial categorizations are a fair reflection of job differences.
They are also invited to an interview in which they provide their
own analysis of the jobs under their supervision.

❏ Time sampling – the question of when to observe and for how
long is also critical. Behaviour may be organized into work-cycles
or events which you will need to identify and represent in your
observations. This may occur if, for example, the processing plant
operates a 'just-in-time' policy (i.e. that there are cycles of work
organized in terms of the purchase order). Moreover, within each
stage of processing there is a series of self-contained work-cycles.
Given the variations in work-cycles, shift managers are invited
to make recommendations about when best to schedule the
observations.

❏ Decide how long each observation should last in order to yield
sufficient information and how many observations it will take to
yield convincing evidence. If evaluating the implementation of an
intervention programme (as well as its outcomes), you will need to
decide at what stage in the programme it is best to observe the
proceedings. In the processing plant, for example, the work-cycles
extend into the night shift. These considerations involve thinking
through issues of both time and event sampling (i.e. what to
observe, when, how often and for how long).

STEP 2: PRODUCE AN OBSERVATION SCHEDULE
The schedule should provide precise indicators of the evidence
being sought, i.e. a system of notation for reporting the following
in relation to the behaviours of interest: frequency (how often),
duration (how long for), exact form (what happened), intensity
(how vigorously), co-occurrence and/or conditions (context). On-
the-spot systems of recording are better than delayed ones. It is

impossible for even a highly experienced observer to remember the exact details of what happened, when and under what conditions. The longer the delay, even if jottings are made at the time, the more room for selective memorization and misinterpretation.

❏ Keep observation items to a minimum to simplify the task and thus help prevent fatigue.

❏ Record behaviours in concrete and specific detail rather than rely on interpretative and impressionistic summary statements.

❏ Develop a system of behavioural notation that is simple to use and remember during the observation process. It will save time and sharpen the observations made.

- The coding system must be manageable. Use as few symbols as possible bearing in mind that you can use the same symbols in different combinations to increase the repertoire of possible behavioural descriptions.

- Design a coding system with view a to subsequent decoding and interpretation. An example is provided below.

METHODS OF RECORDING BEHAVIOUR

This example is taken from a coding and recording sheet for describing staff interactions with children in residential care. Similar designs could be used to code and record other types of work-related behaviours.

Member of staff: .... *Date:* .... *Time commenced:* ....
Number of residents interacted with: ....

Time sampling frame (in minutes)	MO	UI	PVI	PNV	NVI	NNV	IG	Comments
5								
10								
15								
20								
25								
30								

continued

continued —

Recording key:
MO   = Missed observation
UI   = Unclear interaction
PVI   = Positive verbal interaction
PNV = Positive non-verbal interaction
NVI = Negative verbal interaction
NNV = Negative non-verbal interaction
IG   = Ignoring

Coding criteria:

Positive verbal interaction (PVI)
Chatting, praise (e.g. well done, very good, that's better), inviting comment (e.g. what shall we play with, let's sit down and read a story together), supportive comment (e.g. encouragement, reassurance), understanding comment (e.g. 'are you not feeling too happy?')

Positive non-verbal interaction (PNV)
Positive facial expression (smiling, eye contact, engaging), friendly tone, warm/caring gestures and stance (e.g. holding hands, cuddles, stroking hair).

Negative verbal interaction (NVI)
Criticism (e.g. 'No', 'Not like that'), put-down (e.g.'Don't be silly/stupid'), command (e.g. 'Go and wash your hands'), reprimand (e.g. 'You'll do as you're told'; 'I told you not to touch that').

Negative non-verbal interaction (NNV)
Negative facial expression, lack eye contact or staring, threatening/imposing posture and gesture (e.g. shake, smack), negative tone.

Ignoring (IG)
If child makes a request (for help, clarification, information etc.) this is ignored verbally or non-verbally.

❑ Place observation items in a logical sequence; for example, in order of their likely occurrence, time of occurrence or whatever makes sense in relation to whatever is being observed. Since all of the target jobs are organized by work-cycles the observation process is structured accordingly.

❑ Ensure that any observer(s) understand fully any system of notation developed and/or definitions of terms. (Ideally, observers should be coached in the assignment of behavioural codes to ensure reliability.)

❏ Wherever possible use audio/visual support as a check on the reliability of observations. Ask such questions as: How precise is the observation schedule? Would the same kind of evidence be obtained by different observers?

STEP 3: SELECT AND TRAIN THE OBSERVERS
The observers may already be part of the evaluation team or you may need to recruit people specifically for the task. The degree of training they require will vary with how experienced they are, the complexity of events studied and the amount of judgement observers have to make about what they see. Distorted observation arises from:

- Inexperience – the senses become sharper and more acute with practice.

- Fatigue – the observation schedule may be too demanding.

- The interdependence of observation and the inferences made about these observations.

- The interrelatedness of the observer and the situation. The observer may find it difficult to take an impartial stance on a situation in which he or she is involved.

Time permitting, it is advisable that observer(s) are allowed the opportunity to become familiar with the observation schedule and to practise using it. Any difficulties can then be overcome before it really matters. It will also permit a check on the degree of congruence across observers in the notation used to describe the same event.

STEP 4: PREPARE THE PARTICIPANTS
Once the co-operation and commitment of participants is gained they will need to be informed of what exactly is happening, when and for how long. There will be instances where participation is compulsory (according to programme directives), as in the above example. Nonetheless it will aid the process of observation if the trust and respect of those involved is obtained. In our example, the factory operators resisted participation initially. This resistance was understandable: they were not adequately briefed by the programme director (the Human Resources Director) and had surmised that their jobs were in jeopardy (the organization had already been streamlined). They then complained to the trade union representative and the evaluation programme was temporarily stalled. Several meetings were held before the consent

of the trade union representative was gained. But some of the factory operators still expressed resentment at the way in which the initial briefing was handled.

STEP 5: CONDUCT THE OBSERVATIONS

Once accepted, and this may take a while, the issue is one of the influence one might have on the actions of those being observed. Minimize the effects of observation by adopting precautions:

- Be careful not to pass judgement or to adopt a position.

- Spend as much time in the field as possible. The more time spent, the more valid the observations are likely to be.

- Witness a variety of activities. The more varied the activities seen the more likely that the interpretation of observations will be valid.

- Become familiar with the jargon or 'language' of those you are observing. When you do this your observations are likely to be more valid. If necessary (and if possible), check the interpretation of behaviours with participants.

- Be wary of describing events by fitting the observations to a neat categorical scheme. If some of the observations do not 'fit', record them separately. (If necessary, the scheme can be elaborated later to incorporate such observations.)

❏ If a stance of neutrality is impossible it is advisable to become aligned with the programme directives and to remain aloof from any internal disputes that may arise. This will reduce the likelihood of the observer being used as scapegoat for things that could go wrong.

STEP 6: SCORE, INTERPRET AND ANALYSE THE EVIDENCE

Once the unit of observation has been specified (as described in Step 2 above) data handling is relatively straightforward. Measurement in observation is about identifying occurrences (i.e. what, whether and/or how many times something occurs) and the context of these occurrences (what precedes the occurrence, what occurs in parallel, when and where something happens etc.). The form of measurement is likely to be a frequency count of the number of times something happens and in relation to what. Tables describing frequency counts can become complicated unless a clear system of behavioural notation or coding is used.

If it is of interest not just to record the occurrence of something but to describe something and its context (e.g. a behaviour, a style of behaviour, an activity, a procedure, or an event) then precoding is not an issue. In this case, data handling will begin with a detailed analysis of content and the formation of a scheme of categories that summarizes the data in a representative way. The procedure for performing a content analysis is given later under the section on Secondary Sources of Evidence (see page 73). The numerical aspects of data handling is the topic of Chapter 5 to which the reader is referred for guidelines on how next to proceed in the analysis process.

THE OBSERVER AND THE OBSERVATION SITUATION

Observation is something we do all the time. At one extreme is the detached observer who watches from a distance whilst at the other is the observer who is partisan. In practice, the observer will operate in between the two. In-depth insight can by gained by taking on the role of the participants and recreating their everyday thoughts and feelings, although sometimes at the expense of impartiality. For example, on evaluating the impact of a new data handling system on departmental efficiency and effectiveness (e.g. for synthesising information on clinical trials in a pharmaceutical company) it might be appropriate not only to employ various outcome measures but to tap into the reactions of the users on a day-to-day basis. In this way, any anxieties the users have or any problems or difficulties they face in the process of implementing the new system can be identified.

On the other hand, one may be concerned less with the ebb and flow of things than with specific behaviours – in particular the frequency and conditions of their occurrence. Let's say the remit is to evaluate the quality of service provision for children with special needs within a particular health care community. Concern in this situation is mainly with the relationship between the style of behaviour of the carer (i.e. supporting, encouraging/inviting, reprimanding, criticizing or forceful/punitive) and the reactions of the child being handled (e.g. responsive, aggressive, or withdrawing). It is also of interest to identify interactions initiated by the child and the types of reaction they invoke in the carer. In both instances an observation schedule will need to be developed to enable precise sampling of the behaviours which are of interest. In this instance it would be inappropriate for the observer to be 'involved' in the situation.

OBSERVATION: THE PROS AND CONS

'Involved' Observations: Pros
- With the establishment of trust and rapport, your presence as a participating observer may be taken for granted. As a result, people may become less self-conscious and able to behave more 'naturally'.
- You can ask for otherwise 'unintelligible' behaviours to be explained.
- You can gain an in-depth insight into the way of thinking, feeling and behaving of those you are observing.
- As you gain the trust of those involved, you may gain access to information that might otherwise have been carefully guarded.

'Involved' Observation: Cons
- The wealth of information available to you may be overwhelming and unmanageable.
- You may become too involved and thus unable to take an impartial stance on what you are observing.
- You may be side-tracked easily either because of the complexity of the situation and lack of firm observation criteria, and/or through being systematically deflected from the task.
- You may be asked to offer an opinion you are unable to avoid.
- You may be used as 'scapegoat'.
- It is time-consuming.
- There are practical difficulties of writing up your observation notes without being too obvious.
- Observations may become superficial and impressionistic because they are inadequately structured and can be subject to biased interpretation especially if the observer is looking for proof of a particular model or theory.
- The opinions of congenial informants may be given too much weight.

continued

continued —

'Detached' Observation: Pros

- It is focused and standardized and therefore more likely to engender reliable evidence.
- There is less difficulty with remaining 'impartial'.
- It is less time-consuming than 'involved' observation since it is usually more structured and time-bound.
- The information gathered is usually more tangible and specific because it is focused on particular behaviours or sequences of behaviours.

'Detached' Observation: Cons

- It is more difficult to derive information about the context of (or reasons for) a particular behaviour which makes it liable to be misunderstood.
- The presence of the observer(s) can lead to self-consciousness and may alter the behaviour being observed.
- Time is needed to develop the observation criteria and to train the observers if observation is highly prescribed.
- Scheduling problems may arise.
- The timing of the observation may be inappropriate and thus the observations will be atypical. The observations might end up being meaningless abstractions from the daily, monthly or even yearly 'work-cycle' because the time-scale was too short or the entire cycle was not adequately sampled.

Both kinds of observation depend on having obtained the consent of participants including their confidence in the integrity of the observer. Credibility is gained by developing mutual trust and managing people's anxiety about the evaluation process. The extent to which observer presence influences the behaviours of interest is a serious consideration. People become self-conscious and may worry about the consequences of being 'evaluated' for the security of their jobs. Various strategies of self-defence might be employed such as behaving according to perceived expectations rather than the way they normally do or trying to befriend the observers in an attempt to get them to 'take sides'. Consequently the observer is advised to reflect always on the evidence obtained:

- How true is the information gathered?
- Is it an accurate representation of the situation studied?

ASKING QUESTIONS

There are various means of self-report that usefully can be employed by the evaluator and these are encompassed either by the questionnaire or by the interview. Some people are suspicious of the value of these kinds of instruments for gathering evaluation evidence and are reluctant to use them. Ultimately, the appropriateness of the method depends on the purpose of the investigation and the feasibility of identifying more suitable alternatives. The challenge for both the design of the questionnaire and the structure of the interview is to identify the questions that will obtain the most valuable information.

THE QUESTIONNAIRE

A self-completion questionnaire is an instrument requiring responses in writing where people usually indicate their answers with a tick, a circle, a word or a sentence. Most people will have encountered a questionnaire at some point; most often they are mailed - especially if the targets are geographically widespread. However, they might also be distributed by hand. Usually, the questions are in a standardized format – i.e. they are precoded to provide a list of possible responses and are easier to analyse. Use of the questionnaire method involves the following steps:

➤ 1. Produce a sampling plan and a survey timetable.
➤ 2. Develop and send out the questionnaire.
➤ 3. Monitor returns and send out reminder letters.
➤ 4. Handle returned questionnaires.

Each of these steps will be described using an example involving the audit of attitudes of school children towards the 'arts' and the 'sciences', the findings of which will be used to help form local education authority (LEA) policy on science education.

STEP 1: PRODUCE A SAMPLING PLAN AND A SURVEY TIMETABLE
The sampling frame is comprised of all school children between the ages of ten and 16 in all schools under the auspices of one particular LEA. An introductory brief is sent to all relevant schools obliging them to participate in the study. However, it is the responsibility of the programme coordinator to organize its implementation at grass roots. The sampling plan will establish:

- Whether all or only a sample of the schoolchildren will be invited to participate.

- If sampling is required, what strategy will be used and why.

- How many of each age cohort will be involved in the study.

- Classroom details for each age cohort in each of the target schools – e.g. the school, the target class, who the teacher is, how many children in the class, etc.

- Whether the completion of the questionnaire will be compulsory (i.e. conducted during class time) or voluntary (i.e. completed outside school time).

- How the distribution and return of the questionnaires will be organized. Over what time-scale the survey is to be scheduled (including a cut-off date for the return of completed question-naires).

- The schedule in detail once the co-operation and commitment of all relevant parties has been gained, e.g. from school head teachers, class teachers/tutors, the school governors, etc.

STEP 2: DEVELOP AND SEND OUT THE QUESTIONNAIRE
To maximize the likelihood of 'accurate' completion of the questionnaire and its return, it must be skilfully designed with the respondent in mind.

❑ Introduce the questionnaire. State the reason for the questionnaire and explain what will happen with the information in an introductory section:

– The introduction aims to facilitate a maximum number of questionnaires being returned.
– The introduction must provide a clear and brief statement of the purpose and value of the questionnaire. Individuals must be persuaded to respond by some indication of the benefits. It will also need to appeal to their sense of curiosity and worth. A firm but reasonable return date for the questionnaire is established (to include s.a.e. or Freepost for returning the questionnaire). An offer of feedback is given also if this is feasible. An official letterhead and signature adds status and prestige to questionnaires.
– Any necessary assurances of anonymity are also included in the introduction to encourage disclosure. If anonymity cannot be assured, indicate the use(s) to which the information will be put.

– Each questionnaire will need an identification number (or a mailing code for specific groups if applicable) to enable the number of returns to be monitored.

❑ If the questionnaire is divided into sections, ensure that they are appropriately headed. Each section should be briefly introduced and clear instructions for answering questions must be provided. Where necessary illustrate the instructions with a concrete example to minimize any misunderstanding of what is required.

❑ Provide filter questions which give the respondent clear directions of which section to move on to. To aid the filtering procedure, all questions must be numbered by section (e.g. 'If *No* in answer to Section C, Question 8, move on to Section E, Question 1', etc.).

❑ Avoid splitting the questions across pages and give consideration to the design; the page layout and format will influence the willingness of the respondent to complete the questionnaire.

❑ Pose questions that the respondents will perceive as relevant.

❑ Avoid wordiness and ambiguity:
– Write questions in a form which invites the individual to respond rather than which might confuse or intimidate them. When forming a question, anticipate the types of reaction that may arise. Use questions which engage the respondent.
– Choose words and sentences which will be comprehended instantly by the respondent.
– Write questions in a form that makes coding, analysis and interpretation quick and easy.

❑ Pose questions in a logical manner that will make sense to the respondent.

❑ Questions inviting lengthy, open-ended answers are difficult for the respondent to write and for the evaluator to analyse. Where possible, categories of likely responses can be anticipated and offered as alternatives. Answering is more manageable for the respondent in this form and easier for the evaluator to code. If you do want respondents to answer in their own words, pose these question(s) further on in the questionnaire once their interest has been engaged.

❑ If you do provide categories of pre-coded response alternatives, ensure that they are precise (e.g. 'daily', 'two to four times a week', 'once a week') rather than vague (e.g. 'often','sometimes','rarely').

Provide as many alternatives as possible covering all combinations of response. An 'other' category with 'Please state' in parenthesis might also be included.

❑ Avoid questions that could be threatening to respondents – e.g. questions requiring the disclosure of sensitive information, questions which may implicate them in some way or questions which put them in an awkward situation. To some extent this problem can be counteracted by assurances of anonymity.

❑ Pose potentially sensitive questions towards the end of the questionnaire once you are sure that the respondent is engaged. Questions of this kind early on may demotivate the respondent and reduce the likelihood of them completing the rest.

❑ Avoid leading questions – i.e. those which evoke predictable response biases and obscure interpretation. For example a question beginning 'How far would you agree that . . .?' could lead the respondent into agreement.

❑ Keep the evaluation questionnaire as short as possible. A two-page, well-spaced, attractive-looking document is more inviting than a six-page densely-filled one. It should take less than 15 minutes to complete. Finish the questionnaire with a note of thanks.

❑ Where possible, trial the questionnaire using a sample as similar as possible to those to whom it will eventually be sent. Provide space for people to indicate their reactions to certain questions and any recommended changes. Modify, delete or add questions accordingly.

An example of an evaluation questionnaire is given on pages 62–63. This can be regarded as a pro forma for questionnaires designed to evaluate a service of some kind. Substitute for X the name of the particular service provision (or aspect of this) you wish to evaluate.

You may also wish to incorporate an attitude scale into the design of the questionnaire. Steps in developing an attitude scale are provided in the box on pages 64–66 along with examples of different types of attitude scale.

SERVICE EVALUATION QUESTIONNAIRE FOR CONSUMERS

The information sought by this questionnaire is designed to provide evidence for the effectiveness of X from a user's point of view. This evidence is important because we need to know whether the services we provide are meeting users' needs. As a user of X, you are invited to complete the questions below as openly and as honestly as you can. Your views and those of other users will be used to make recommendations for change. Altogether these questions should take you no longer than ten minutes to complete. First we need you to provide a few basic details about yourself which will help us to make sense of what you say about X:

Are you MALE or FEMALE? (Please circle)   MALE   FEMALE

How old are you?   .... YEARS OLD

When was the last time you used X?
                    DATE .... MONTH .... YEAR

How often have you used X? (please indicate how many times)
                              .... TIMES

Occupation/profession (please state) ....

What was your main objective in using X? ....

To what extent do you think that X was effective in meeting this objective? (Please circle one of the following on the scale below).

Excellent – all aspects of X effective	Good – most aspects of X effective	Adequate – met minimum expectations	Poor – room for consider- able improve- ment

If mostly 'good' which aspects of X would you say were most effective ? (Please indicate with a tick which of any number of things were effective).

- X itself (the event and the activities involved).   ☐
- The way X was delivered (methods, procedures).   ☐
- The timing of X (when it took place).   ☐
- The people who delivered X (attitudes, behaviours, skills, competence).   ☐
- The administrative arrangements relating to X (how well organized and administered).   ☐
- The duration of X (how long it took).   ☐
- Where X took place (the location and environment of X).   ☐
- Other (please state):   ☐

....

....

....

continued

continued –

Please indicate with a tick, which of the following characteristics you reckon were 'poor' or 'only adequate':

- X itself (the event and the activities involved). ☐
- The way X was delivered (methods, procedures). ☐
- The timing of X (when it took place). ☐
- The people who delivered X (attitudes, behaviours, skills, competence). ☐
- The administrative arrangements relating to X (how well organized and administered). ☐
- The duration of X (how long it took). ☐
- Where X took place (the location and environment of X). ☐
- Other (please state): ☐

....
....
....

Please tell us why you think that these things are 'poor' or 'only adequate':

....
....
....

What do you think might be done to improve the effectiveness of X ? (Please tick any or all of the following):

- Rethink the event itself and the activities it involves. ☐
- Change the methods or procedures used in implementing X. ☐
- Change the timing of X. ☐
- Reassess staff competence in administering X. ☐
- Clarify staff roles in implementing X. ☐
- Reassess the administrative arrangements relating to X. ☐
- Increase the duration of X. ☐
- Decrease the duration of X. ☐
- Change the pace of X. ☐
- Change the location or environment of X. ☐
- Other (please state): ☐

....
....
....

Please explain what exactly you would do to make the kinds of improvements you have indicated and why ?

....
....
....

Any other comments about X?

....
....
....

ATTITUDE SCALES

An attitude refers to someone's predisposition to act in a certain way or to endorse a particular point of view. An attitude can never be accessed directly; it can only be measured through the way it is expressed (i.e. by what people say and do). To elicit an attitude people can be invited to indicate the extent of their agreement or disagreement with a set of statements about a particular issue. These statements form an attitude scale. The degree of an individual's possession of whatever attitude the scale claims to measure is indicated by grading the extent of agreement/disagreement with each statement (e.g. 1 for Strongly Agree, 2 for Agree..n). The numerical rule used depends on the particular type of attitude scale being employed (see below for examples of two different types). The scale is always made up of a series of verbal statements which are assumed to reflect one underlying theme. One statement is unlikely to be a satisfactory indicator of an attitude on its own. For example, we may be asked to monitor changes in employees' commitment to 'total quality' principles and practices following the introduction of employee participation procedures (e.g. 'quality circles'). Attitude scales can be used with any method of data collection; two different types are described below:

THE LIKERT SCALE
A set of attitude statements is rated on a five-point scale (i.e. strongly agree, agree, undecided, disagree strongly, disagree). The attitude is then said to be the sum of an individual's ratings across the statements. For example:

'Performance related pay will facilitate employee commitment to their work.'

Strongly agree	Agree	Undecided	Disagree	Strongly disagree
1	2	3	4	5

THE SEMANTIC DIFFERENTIAL
This is designed to measure the meaning of an attitude object, i.e. its affective or evaluative significance. The semantic differential has three components:

1. The attitude object which is to be evaluated. (For example, a training programme designed to enhance employees' knowledge of a new corporate plan.)

2. A series of adjective pairs which anchor the scale in terms of polar opposites. (The success of the training programme in getting the message across for example may be assessed using the following adjective pairs to tap the theme of 'understandability':)

— - *continued* —

— -*continued* —

Predictable	_:_:_:_:_:_:_	Unpredictable
Understandable	_:_:_:_:_:_:_	Incomprehensible
Familiar	_:_:_:_:_:_:_	Strange
Simple	_:_:_:_:_:_:_	Complicated
Clear	_:_:_:_:_:_:_	Confusing

3. A scale of measurement. The adjective pairs are anchored by a seven-point scale of measurement. Note that each of the scale points are undefined. In responding to the scale, individuals mark a cross in the box which they feel most closely represents how they feel about the training programme in question.

The adjective pairs are chosen according to the purpose of the research and the nature of the attitude object being evaluated.

Developing a Likert Scale:
The following steps describe the development of a popular form of attitude scale.

Step 1: Define the attitude it is necessary to have evidence of. The example used refers to an attitude of 'commitment to total quality principles and practices'.

Step 2: Check the availability of existing attitude scales tapping into the kind of evidence required. There are lots of scales which claim to measure 'organizational commitment' but none (that we know of) that tap into commitment in the more specific sense defined here.

Step 3: Collect statements which are presumed to reflect the attitude in question.
– What kinds of verbal statements will provide relevant evidence of attitude?
– Brainstorm ideas and invite other people (who are not involved in the evaluation) to suggest possible statements.

Step 4: Form a response scale on which a range of reactions from positive to negative can be recorded.
– The scale may indicate level of agreement/disagreement, like/dislike, acceptance/rejection, importance/unimportance.
– Typically a five-point or seven-point scale is used as the form of measurement.

Ensure each point on the scale is clearly and unambiguously labelled. More than seven points on a scale requires fine discrimination in judgement which may be difficult to handle. This may lead people to be fairly arbitrary in their patterns of response. Less than five points on a scale may not capture the range of differences likely to be expressed in judgements and may lead people to insert their own scale point which best reflects what they think (or to omit responding altogether). A three-point scale, for example, will capture only very global responses and

— — — — — — — — — — — — — — — — — — — - *continued* —

— continued —

will tend to bias people into using the middle point of the scale to avoid making what they feel to be an overly definitive judgement.

Step 5: Distribute the attitude scales to a small sample of people not involved in the study for a trial run. The trial sample would need to be as similar as possible to the target sample (e.g. employees in another company which operates according the total quality principles). This, however, may be neither practical or feasible. If it is not possible, move on to Step 6.

Step 6: Construct the attitude scale. Identify the key attitude statements to be included in the final scale. Edit them in terms of their wording and their range of coverage. In the example provided there are two attitude objects, thus it is advisable to produce separate scales (e.g. one to access commitment to total quality principles and one to access commitment to total quality practices).

– The attitude statements should be worded clearly and unambiguously.

– The instructions administered must also be clear and concise. Where possible an illustration of how to respond to the attitude scale should be provided which takes care not to lead individuals into a particular way of responding.

– Define the scale points to capture a range of responses.

STEP 3: MONITOR RETURNS AND SEND OUT REMINDER LETTERS

Monitor the return rate of the questionnaires. Target non-returns by sending a reminder letter a few days after the deadline. This should imply that the individual intends to complete and return the questionnaire but had perhaps forgotten to do so. The importance of the study will need to be reaffirmed as well as the value of any contribution to it.

STEP 4: HANDLE RETURNED QUESTIONNAIRES

Since the answers provided in questionnaires are pre-coded it is relatively easy to translate them into a numerical form. Chapter 5 describes the procedures for handling this data. For now it is important to note the percentage of questionnaires returned. If the return rate is low (e.g. less than 40 per cent) you will need to consider how far you can generalize from your sample to a wider population.

The main considerations in deciding whether or not to use the questionnaire method are listed in the box below.

QUESTIONNAIRES: THE PROS AND CONS

Pros
- They provide answers to a variety of standard questions. They can be answered anonymously.
- A large number of people can be surveyed relatively cheaply.
- Standardized and pre-coded questions speed up the process of analysis and interpretation.
- They allow the respondent time to think before answering.
- They can be given to many people who are geographically widely dispersed simultaneously.
- Uniformity and standardization: once the survey has begun, the questions cannot be changed since the aim is to produce comparable information.

Cons
- They rely on recollections of behaviour some time after their occurrence.
- They are apt to be left uncompleted and unreturned. Some people find it difficult to express themselves by questionnaire.
- They are apt to be sent back only partially completed or with illegible or incomprehensible replies.
- Standardization of the questions does not ensure uniformity of interpretation.
- Resistances can be engendered if threatening/sensitive questions are asked or if respondents are forced to choose between a constrained set of answers.

THE INTERVIEW

An interview is a face-to-face meeting between two or more people in which the respondent answers questions in a structured, semi-structured or unstructured way. In the structured form the questions are predetermined as in a questionnaire whereas in the unstructured form the interviewer is free to pursue a line of questioning around a particular topic or criterion. The latter is typical in counselling-style interviews. Here we focus on the interview as a 'semi-structured' device: the evaluation interview is structured by a series of predetermined questions but the interviewer is free to pursue lines of enquiry sparked by the responses obtained. The degree of structure necessary will depend on how factual is the information sought. If detailed answers are required then it may be necessary to use probing questions to facilitate this. The objective may be best met without imposing too much structure on the respondents' answers. This also means, however, that the interview is more susceptible to bias. Steps will therefore need to be taken to minimize this. The interview can be used as:

- A tool for obtaining particular types of information not easily obtained by alternative or better means.

- An exploratory device to help identify key issues to guide another phase of the research.

- A supplement to other methods; for example, to follow up unexpected results obtained by other methods, to validate the information obtained by other methods, to go deeper into the motivations of respondents and their reasons for acting as they do.

- A tool for inviting children (who are unlikely to be able to respond to questionnaires without adult help) to offer their thoughts and feelings on certain issues.

- A tool for inviting illiterate/semi-literate people to offer their views in a less threatening way.

- A tool for inviting people from various ethnic backgrounds to offer their views in a less standardized and less prescriptive linguistic form.

Use of the interview method involves the following steps:

➢ Define the purpose of the interview.
➢ Plan the sampling strategy and timetable the interviews.
➢ Develop the interview schedule and build into this a method for handling information.
➢ Conduct the interviews.
➢ Analyse and interpret the interview data.

The example used to illustrate the steps involved derives from the case of the processing plant described earlier (see page 49). Interviews are conducted with a sample of factory operators and shift managers to complement the 'job analysis' information obtained by observation. The following steps are taken:

STEP 1: DEFINE THE PURPOSE OF THE INTERVIEW

In the example, the purpose of the interview was to obtain information about the following aspects of the job:

Procedures/Tasks: What tasks do operators need to perform as part of their job?

Job Knowledge: What do operators need to know in order to perform the job to standard?

Job Skill: What particular skills do operators need to acquire in order to perform the job to standard?

Job Related Attributes: What particular qualities/attributes does an operator need to have in order to perform the job to standard?

Job Context: Under what particular conditions is the job performed?

STEP 2: PLAN THE SAMPLING STRATEGY AND TIMETABLE THE INTERVIEWS

❏ In the example all the factory operators observed as part of the evaluation are invited to participate in a 40-minute interview. Since their attendance is compulsory it is difficult to judge the degree of true co-operation and commitment secured. The interviews are scheduled to follow the observation exercise. An introductory letter is sent to each participant explaining the purpose of the interviews and to what use the information will be put, who will be conducting them, where they will take place, and for how long. They are also assured of the confidentiality of their particular replies although it is noted that they would be used to produce an official job evaluation report available for public circulation. This is an important qualifier to the confidentiality clause.

❏ All six shift managers are also invited to participate in a 40-minute, one-to-one interview. The introductory letter explains that their help is needed to provide important back-up information about the jobs under their supervision.

❏ Interviews with the operators are scheduled by the shift managers who then also indicate their own availability for interview. All interviews are conducted during paid overtime. In this way, little disruption is caused to the running of the plant. Moreover, operators can feel that at least there is some reward for the time and effort involved.

❏ Interviews are scheduled in the Training Centre – i.e. on fairly neutral ground. Note that interviews conducted in the Director's office or other location signifying interviewer status and power might intimidate the respondent.

STEP 3: DEVELOP THE INTERVIEW SCHEDULE

❏ The aims of the interview need to be translated into specific questions. The form of interview questions and their ordering should follow the questionnaire guidelines provided on page 59. The difference (compared with written responses) lies in the flexibility afforded by the interview. Suitable probing questions can be prepared either in advance of the interview or can be formulated during it, as and when required.

❏ If potentially sensitive questions are asked the use of prompt cards containing labelled response alternatives (A, B, C...etc) can help to minimize the potential for engendering any threat or embarrassment.

❏ A method of recording interview responses will also need to be devised. Writing down each response verbatim can interrupt the flow of interviews. On the other hand, scribbled notes may be unintelligible later. Ideally, the interviews are audio-taped and transcribed. Not only is this more convenient, it may enhance the credibility of the interview process. However, always seek the permission of the interviewee first.

STEP 4: CONDUCT THE INTERVIEWS

Always use an introduction:

➤ Reiterate the purpose of the interview.

➤ Outline the agenda of the *interview.*

➤ Indicate how long it will take.

➤ Make the interviewee feel that their contribution is special and highly valued.

➤ Provide the opportunity for the interviewee to ask questions.

➤ Put the interviewee at ease right from the start by assuming a relaxed, open and friendly manner.

➤ Ask permission for the interview to be audio-taped (if this is to be done).

The following points need to be taken into consideration when working through the interview schedule:

• Follow the sequence of questions section-by-section.

- Frame questions in a language that ensures effective communication and omit any ambiguous or abstract vocabulary.
- Ensure that the interviewee appreciates the purpose of each question to avoid arousing suspicion or resistance.
- When probing or seeking clarification take care not to put words into the interviewee's mouth.
- Use probes like 'Tell me more about . . .' or subtle prompts like 'Go on . . .' or even an expectant silence.
- Use leading questions only if it will evoke a more reflective response than a more straightforward question.
- Avoid hypothetical questions such as 'What if you were to . . .' or 'What would you do if . . .' which lead to hypothetical answers.
- Be alert to your own influence as the interviewer on what the interviewee says, i.e. by your tone of voice, posture, style of questioning, etc.

Conclude the interview
➤ Invite the interviewee to add anything they think is relevant or to ask questions. Take care not to assume a particular position by agreeing with the interviewee or offering comments.
➤ Thank the interviewee for their time and contribution.

STEP 5: TRANSCRIBE THE INTERVIEW
Transcribing interviews verbatim is time-consuming and laborious unless there is money available to pay someone else to do it (e.g. audio-tape transcription services). Furthermore, full transcription may not be necessary. It is inadvisable to quote verbatim from interviews in which you have provided assurances of confidentiality. Experience has shown that distinctive quotes are readily traceable to their source, particularly in small-scale organizations where many of the employees are well known and have characteristic ways of expressing themselves.

STEP 6: SCORE, ANALYSE AND INTERPRET THE INTERVIEW DATA
Closed answers to interview questions may be pre-coded (e.g. Yes=1, No=2 etc.). The more open-ended answers will need to be coded by applying content analysis (see the next section on Secondary Sources of Evidence). Refer to Chapter 5 for details on how to analyse the numerical data derived from the content analysis.

The main considerations in deciding whether or not to use the interview method are listed in the box below.

INTERVIEWS: THE PROS AND CONS

Pros

Information can be obtained from people who cannot read, who have difficulty understanding certain question wordings or who find it difficult to concentrate.

- They permit flexibility and allow the interviewer to pursue unanticipated lines of inquiry.
- They permit probing and clarification to obtain more complete and in-depth information.
- They make it possible for rapport to be established and maintained with the respondent.
- They provide a means of checking and assuring the effectiveness of communication between respondent and interviewer.

Cons

- They are time consuming, costly and sometimes inconvenient.
- Sometimes the interviewer can unduly influence the responses of the interviewee.
- The interviewee may be apt to provide rationalisations (i.e. socially desirable and logical reasons) for their actions rather than the 'real' ones in order to meet perceived expectations.
- Different answers can be obtained depending on the perceived status/power of the interviewer. For example, a high status and powerful interviewer recognizable to all within the organization may obtain 'favourable' responses to questions concerned with eliciting reactions to certain changes (e.g. the introduction of compulsory in-service training) whilst 'negative' responses (i.e. criticisms and complaints) may be obtained by a low status interviewer who has limited power.
- Retrospective information about behaviour may be under- or over-reported due to memory lapses or in order to present a particular self-image.

_ continued _

continued –

- Interviews require skill: misdirected probing could alienate the interviewee.
- Responses are more difficult to record and analyse.
- Some interviewees may find it difficult to describe their thoughts and feelings in their own words.

SECONDARY SOURCES OF EVIDENCE

A source of information that is not compiled for evaluation purposes but which may throw light on the issues concerned is termed a secondary rather than a primary source. For example, you may be required to evaluate the effectiveness of a change programme that has already occurred. In this case, the main source of evidence concerns the actual outcomes obtained. However, in order to identify the origins of certain effects you may also need to obtain information about how exactly the programme was implemented, i.e. not just a formal specification but information about the programme in action. Consequently, any records that were kept during the implementation process (e.g. of the materials used or the activities involved) will be useful sources of evidence to complement that obtained, say, by interview with those involved. Once the objectives of the evaluation exercise have been clarified the main question to ask is: 'How can I make the most effective use of existing records?'. Some types of secondary sources of evidence pertinent to evaluation are listed below:

Expressive documents	*Mass media reports*	*Official documents*
e.g. letters	e.g. local newspapers	e.g. employee records

Steps in the use of secondary sources of evidence are as follows:

STEP 1: IDENTIFY WHAT KINDS OF RECORDS HAVE BEEN KEPT AND THEIR AVAILABILITY
For example, letters, logbooks, terms of reference, policy or mission statements.

STEP 2: PREPARE A SAMPLING PLAN FOR COLLECTING THE RECORDS
➤ Identify which records you will need and why.
➤ Negotiate access to the records.
➤ Produce a time schedule.

STEP 3: ESTABLISH RECORD AUTHENTICITY
Check the plausibility and consistency of the records. Systematic falsification of records is rare but biases are in-built. Where possible Identify the authorship and the purpose of the document. Ask:

❑ How complete are the records? Are there any obvious omissions? Are there any patterns discernible in the type of omissions identified?

❑ How credible is the information gleaned from the document? Does it make sense? How does it compare with information derived from other sources of documentation?

❑ Is there an ulterior agenda discernible in the particular content and style of the documentation?

❑ For whom was the document written? Why was it written?

STEP 4: APPLY CONTENT ANALYSIS TO THE RECORDS
Content analysis is the generic term for managing non-numerical information. Mostly this is done by forming categories which help initially in making more sense of the information obtained. These categories enable the data to be described and inferences to be drawn.

Content analysis involves a mechanical as well as an interpretative component. The mechanical aspect involves transcription (i.e. from taped interviews) as well as the organization and subdivision of the data into categories. The interpretative component involves determining what categories are meaningful in terms of the questions being asked. Sometimes the observation or interview schedule can be used as the starting point here. However, there are instances where the evaluator must start completely from scratch as in, for example, an attempt to reconstruct a particular event in the analysis of secondary sources of data. The mechanical and the interpretative component are inextricably linked insofar as it necessitates a cyclical process back and forth between the transcripts/records and the conceptualization (i.e. how the content of these is conceptualized to check the relevance and interpretability of the categorical scheme).

There are a few points to bear in mind when performing content analysis:

• Any form of editing during transcription is inadvisable. Owing to the time-consuming and laborious nature of transcription, it is tempting to analyse the content directly from the tape. This kind of **selective transcription** risks clouding the entire character of any interview or series of interviews from which themes can be discerned. Moreover, it would not be very easy for someone else to check the reliability and validity of a category scheme derived in this way.

- The cutting, sorting and the cyclical process of conceptualization can be unwieldy. There are computer-assisted approaches to data reduction which are designed to make at least the mechanics of the task much more manageable.

- Look not only for what is said but also what is not said. Sometimes issues are strategically side-stepped and can thus be very telling.

- Always make the rules of data reduction explicit so that others are given the opportunity to check the reliability and validity of your interpretative scheme for themselves.

STEP 5: DEVELOP A CODING SCHEME FOR HANDLING THE DATA
If you wish to quantify data which has been analysed for content you will need to develop a suitable coding scheme. This will enable you then to perform a frequency count of the number of instances in the data that fall into each particular category. This will enable you to get a feel for how important certain categories are relative to others. It might also be possible to perform some simple statistics (see Chapter 5, especially the box on page 89). Alternatively, you may be more interested in how the data can be characterized in terms of the particular content of the categories you have produced. For example, you might examine a series of historical documents for how 'normal' childhood is portrayed and the implications of this for workplace policy in caring for children with special learning difficulties. In this case coding and quantification is irrelevant. The main considerations in deciding whether or not to use secondary sources of evidence are listed in the box overleaf.

SECONDARY SOURCES OF EVIDENCE:
THE PROS AND CONS

Pros

- A rich source of information obtained with minimal effort, time and money.

- A contemporaneous rather than retrospective source of evidence.

- Can be used to validate retrospective evidence.

- Records are made without the objective of evaluation in mind and should be relatively free from bias.

- Can be used to provide context information. For example, the analysis of relevant press cuttings pertaining to the object of evaluation (e.g. expanding an existing motorway or the management of industrial waste) may enable the evaluator to put the project in the context of local reactions as represented by the media.

Cons

- The process of examining documents/records and abstracting relevant information can be time-consuming.

- Programme records may be incomplete, difficult to decipher and may reflect the agenda of the individual(s) who made them.

- There may be ethical and legal constraints involved in gaining access and/or examining certain records.

Chapter 5 pursues the topic of how to handle quantified data using simple descriptive and inferential statistics.

Handling Evaluation Information: Analysis of Data

In the introductory chapter we noted that the purpose of evaluation should be to tell you whether what is happening is producing the results you want. It may also, on occasion, go further and attempt to establish how and why these results are achieved. Evaluation is fundamentally an analytic activity. In Chapters 3 and 4 various designs and data elicitation techniques were presented. Although various issues of measurement were discussed the analytic process itself – the process of data handling and interpretation – has yet to be described.

Understanding how to analyse evaluation data is the key to producing valid conclusions. This chapter presents ways of describing numerical information and shows how to test inferences which enable valid conclusions to be drawn. In particular, it ties the presentation of methods of data reduction and inference testing to the design types described in Chapter 3. Each design type is considered separately. Design and analysis are interrelated: it is inadvisable to plan to use a particular design without considering how inferences can be drawn to reach useful conclusions.

In instances where the data are not yet in numerical form guidelines are provided on how to convert it. Each example will be accompanied by a consideration of the inherent weaknesses and difficulties of the approach illustrated. The description of information handling techniques is limited to the simplest kind statistically but nevertheless the reader is informed of other more powerful methods which they might like or need to have at their finger tips.

THE BASIC DATA HANDLING MODEL

ASSESSING IMPACT WITH GAIN SCORE ANALYSIS

All instances of evaluation, whatever the method used, require some systematic consideration of whether certain things are having the impact desired. To simplify matters the event of interest will be treated as the 'cause' and the post-event measurements as the 'outcome'. The issue in this instance is to identify the causal impact of the event as reflected in the outcome measure(s). Exactly how the impact is assessed will vary with the design. Generally speaking however, impact is assessed using some form of '**gain score analysis**'. This involves determining the extent to which the measures obtained from the treatment group *after* the event, are an improvement on those obtained *before* it occurred. For example, we would like to be able to say that nurses who participated in a workshop on AIDS/HIV expressed more positive attitudes towards caring for the patient with HIV than before. In other words, the impact of the event is assessed against the starting point as yardstick – in this example, negative base-line attitudes towards caring for the patient with HIV.

OBTAINING A VALID YARDSTICK WITH GAIN SCORE ANALYSIS

The before-and-after comparison in gain score analysis may or may not be made by taking into consideration the difference in scores obtained by a group which was not involved in the event of interest, or against some pre-determined standard. (For example, the attitudes of nurses who did not participate in the workshop on AIDS/HIV towards caring for patients with HIV compared with a conceptual model defining good nursing care.) In some designs (e.g. the Now-and-then Design) 'gain' can only be assessed by comparing the scores obtained from the treatment group with those obtained from a comparison group reckoned to be equivalent in all respects except their exposure to the event in question. Certain assumptions are then made about the 'starting point' of each of the groups (e.g. negative attitudes towards caring for patients with HIV). The various designs differ in the types of yardstick that are used to analyse gain. Later in the chapter it will be demonstrated that it is the quality of the yardstick which determines how confident one can be in making assertions about the impact of an event.

ASSESSING IMPACT BY INVESTIGATING RELATIONSHIPS

On occasion, it may not be possible to assess impact by analysing gain scores. The evaluations using the Now Design, for example, might not always yield the kind of information that is conducive to this kind of analysis. There are also instances where it is actually not the most appropriate form of analysis, at least not in itself. It may be of more interest – either *per se* or in addition to gain score analysis – to investigate relationships. Chapter 3 noted the importance of considering process factors as well as outcomes in order to ascertain what particular features of an event are responsible for producing the outcomes obtained. It is often not enough simply to assert that the event worked, or otherwise; we may need to know exactly what it was about the event that produced (or that prevented it from having) the predicted effect. Let's say that you have obtained evidence that shop floor industry workers are more likely to demonstrate 'commitment to quality' if they work in an organization which invites employee participation rather than one which does not. This raises the question of both how and why employee participation has this effect.

CONCEPTUAL MODELS IN GUIDING PROCESS

Guidance in answering questions of 'why' and 'how' may be provided by a conceptual model or set of assumptions underpinning the impact of the study to be tested out. The only limit to this is the amount and type of evidence available which relies in part on having the foresight to build considerations of process into the evaluation at the outset. Without the guidance of a conceptual model of some kind, however, it would be difficult to know what to look for, let alone how to measure it. There are various forms of relationship analysis that enable process factors to be elucidated. This chapter guides you through a very simple form of relationship analysis using concrete examples and, at the same time, pointing you in the direction of other more powerful techniques that build on this. First, some ways of describing and summarizing evaluation data are demonstrated and explained.

DESCRIBING AND SUMMARIZING DATA

Impact analysis relies on the data being presented in a manageable form, rather than just a complex array of individual scores. It is also important to be able to discern patterns in the data simply by inspection. Various statistics are available which enable you to describe and summarize your data as a) an aid to discerning patterns and b) as a foundation for testing inferences about, and interpreting, these patterns.

DETERMINING THE CENTRAL TENDENCY IN THE DISTRIBUTION OF DATA

A measure of **central tendency** provides a score which is the most representative of all the scores obtained in a sample. It is the central point of the data and how it is distributed across a measurement scale. One important measure of central tendency – the **sample mean** – is the arithmetical average of a set of scores, which is obtained by adding the scores together and then dividing by the total number of scores in the set. A set of scores is defined by their group of origin (e.g. treatment group, comparison group) as well as the time of elicitation (i.e. pre-event/post-event). The mean calculation for all forms of gain score analysis requires that you compute the sample mean for each group of people and, where relevant, at each particular point in time. Thus, the table below provides the

Table 5.1 The reading scores and sample means for two groups of children

	Group 1 (treatment)		Group 2 (comparison)	
	Pre-event	Post-event	Pre-event	Post-event
	4.5	7.8	4.0	4.1
	4.7	4.6	4.5	4.4
	4.2	6.8	4.4	4.8
	4.9	5.0	5.0	5.2
	3.6	6.1	4.3	4.6
	5.1	4.0	3.9	4.0
	3.8	4.7	4.0	3.8
sum	30.8	39.0	30.1	30.9
mean	4.4	5.6	4.3	4.4

Answers

	Group 1 (treatment)		Group 2 (comparison)	
	Pre-event	*Post-event*	*Pre-event*	*Post-event*
	sd = 2.26	sd = 3.72	sd = 2.46	sd = 2.36

mean scores for both treatment and comparison groups at both pre- and post-event on the outcome measure of interest, in this case the mean scores of two groups of children on a reading test, before and after the teaching event of interest.

The scores obtained for Group 1 pre-event presented in the table will be used as an example. The sum of all the scores in this column is 30.8. If this is divided by 7 – the total number of scores in the set – the mean is 4.4. Simply from this table of means you can see that a) the treatment group has obtained a higher mean score after the teaching event than before it, with a difference of 1.2; b) that the scores for the comparison group who were not exposed to the teaching intervention did not change much (difference = 0.1); even though c) the treatment and comparison groups obtained comparable scores at the outset (difference = 0.1). Therefore it would be tempting to infer that the event was successful because those who were exposed to the teaching event improved in their reading ability whilst those who were not exposed did not. However this would be totally unjustified unless we had some way of knowing whether the difference obtained is a 'trustworthy' one or whether it could easily have occurred by chance. Fundamental to inference testing is being able to identify and explain the amount of variation in the data.

IDENTIFYING THE AMOUNT OF VARIATION IN THE DATA

Measures of variation tell us whether the scores in a set cluster closely around their average or whether they scatter widely. These measures are concerned with the spread of scores in a distribution and can reveal how representative the average is. If the variation is small it can be assumed that all the individual scores are close to it. If the variation is large, then the mean is unlikely to be a true and representative way of characterizing the data. For instance, it would be inappropriate to infer that improvement occurred amongst a group of children exposed to a teaching event if, as in the table above, they varied widely in their reading scores. The teaching event may well appear to be successful overall (according to the pattern of means) but if you look closely at the degree of variation in post-event reading scores it is clear that, whilst three children do indeed show a lot of improvement in their reading ability, three children show very little improvement and one child actually appears to get worse!

In the table below, two sets of scores are represented, both of which have the same mean of 75 yet they exhibit clearly different degrees of variation. The scores of all the students in Class 1 are clustered close to the mean whereas the scores of students in Class 2 are spread over a wide range. Some measure is required to describe exactly how these two distributions differ.

Table 5.2 An illustration of differences in the spread of scores

Class 1	73	74	75	76	77	(mean=75)
Class 2	60	65	75	85	90	(mean=75)

One such measure is known as the '**range**'. The range is the spread between the highest and the lowest score which, for Class 1, is 4 (i.e. the difference between 73 and 77) and for Class 2 is 30 (i.e. 60–90). Although easy to compute, the range is a rather crude measure which takes account only of the most extreme scores of the distribution. It is a useful measure for describing the particular characteristics of the sample. For example, it would be used to say that the children in Class 1 ranged in age from 6 years 1 month to 7 years 3 months. It is less useful if the measurement scale used does not make much sense across different samples and contexts.

A more sensitive measure which takes account of every score and which is the basis for inference testing, is known as the **standard deviation (SD)**. Specifically the SD measures how far each score making up a distribution 'deviates' from that distribution's mean. The deviation (d) of each score from the mean is computed and squared; then the average of these squared values is obtained. The SD is the square root of this average written as a formula:

$$SD = \frac{\text{sum of each deviation squared}}{\text{Number of cases in sample}}$$

Specimen computation of the standard deviation

Class 1	d	d^2	Class 2	d	d^2
77–75	2	4	90–75	15	225
76–75	1	1	85–75	10	100
75–75	0	0	75–75	0	0
74–75	−1	1	65–75	−10	100
73–75	−2	4	60–75	−15	225
sum		10	sum		650

mean of d^2 = 10/5 = 2.0   mean of d^2 = 650/5 = 130
sd = $\sqrt{2.0}$ = 1.4   sd = $\sqrt{130}$ = 11.4

Using the data sets presented in table 5.2, an example of how to compute the standard deviation is given. The steps in the computation are given below:

Step 1: Subtract the mean score from each individual score as shown above to produce a 'deviation' score (d). A positive d value is yielded if the score is above the mean and a negative d value is yielded if the score is below the mean.

Step 2: Each d value is squared. Any minus signs will now disappear.

Step 3: The squared deviations are added (sum) and then divided by N – the total number of scores in the sample (mean of d^2) which in this example is 5.

Step 4: The square root of the mean of d^2 produces the standard deviation (sd).

You can see from this analysis that the standard deviations differ substantially for each of these data sets even though they have the same mean. You will need to be able to compute the standard deviation in order to use gain score analysis.

Before you move on, it is suggested that you compute the standard deviations for each of the data sets in the table 5.1. Once you feel comfortable with this way of describing and summarizing data, you are ready to consider the process of interpretation: the drawing of inferences from data.

DRAWING INFERENCES

EVALUATION RESEARCH ALWAYS DEALS WITH SAMPLES

It is very rare to have access to the total population of people in a certain category. Even if it was possible no doubt it would be impractical to obtain measurements from every single member. Instead the aim is to represent it by drawing a sample from it. More often than not in evaluation research the sample is not randomly drawn but is what might be termed a **'convenience sample'** (e.g. a class of children, or care workers in a particular day nursery) or a **'quota sample'** i.e. people selected because of some characteristic they have in common (e.g. all females in a particular catchment area who have not attended a local clinic for breast screening).

SAMPLING INEVITABLY INTRODUCES ERROR

If a researcher was to draw several samples from the same population they would obtain slightly different results due to the fact that the sample does not fully represent the whole population and thus contains 'errors' of sampling. This is where statistical inference comes into play. A sample yields data from which it is possible to make inferences about the population as a whole. If the sample has not been drawn randomly from the population there is much more chance of introducing **sampling error**. This is something that applied research must always contend with and often undermines its potential to produce findings that can be generalized to the population as a whole.

TAKING ACCOUNT OF SAMPLING ERROR

Statistical inference is always made under some degree of uncertainty due to sampling error. If statistical tests indicate that the magnitude of the effect found in the sample is fairly large relative to the estimate of sampling error then you can be more confident that the effect observed in the sample holds for the population at large. So, statistical inference deals with the problem of making an inference or judgement about some feature of a population based solely on information obtained from a sample of that population. In order to test inferences it is crucial to be able to compute the mean, the standard deviation and the standard error of the mean. It has been shown already how to compute the mean and the standard deviation; now that you are equipped with some basic statistical concepts and techniques you can move on to consider how they might be used to draw inferences about the significance of gain scores – i.e. the testing of the significance of differences.

TESTING THE SIGNIFICANCE OF DIFFERENCES

When data are collected on two groups where one is exposed to an event whilst the other is not, it is of interest to see whether their mean test results differ in any systematic way. In table 5.1 we presented the reading scores obtained for two groups of children both before and after a teaching event designed to improve the reading ability of those who comprised the treatment group. Whilst the mean scores appeared to differ in the way predicted (i.e. the treatment group produced a higher mean score after the event than before it), it was pointed out that it would be unjustified to make assertions about the impact of the event without ruling out the possibility that the improvement apparent in the data could have arisen by chance. It was noted also that there was wide variation in reading scores obtained by the treatment group post-event. It is quite possible that a few extreme scores (i.e. the few who showed big gains in scores) could easily have produced overall differences between groups. In other words, the difference obtained between pre- and post-event might not be very reliable. This means that if the study were to be repeated, it is unlikely that the results would be the same. Many chance factors could give rise to the differences. By using statistical tests you will be able judge the likelihood of the differences being true ones – i.e. due to the effect of the intervention – rather than the product of random error.

Another example illustrating the problem of drawing inferences about the significance of differences between means is given in the table below. You will see that the differences between means is the same (i.e. 8 points difference). However Data set 2 indicates a more reliable difference between means than Data set 1.

Table 5.3 A comparison of the reliability of two data sets

Example Data set 1

Treatment group		Comparison group	
Person	*Score*	*Person*	*Score*
1	40	1	40
2	45	2	45
3	50	3	50
4	55	4	55
5	100	5	60
sum	290	sum	250
mean	58	mean	50

Example Data set 2

Treatment group		Comparison group	
Person	*Score*	*Person*	*Score*
1	56	1	48
2	57	2	49
3	58	3	50
4	59	4	51
5	60	5	52
sum	290	sum	250
mean	58	mean	50

The wider the variation in individual scores within each of the groups the less confident one can be in asserting the significance of the difference between means. Statistical tests of inference provide a precise way to determine the reliability of the mean differences. The examples provided so far illustrate that the significance of a difference will depend on both the size of the obtained difference and the variability of the scores being compared. But this is not the place to show you how to perform statistical tests on your data. Instead, some of the tests that can be employed will be discussed by referring back to each of the evaluation designs outlined in Chapter 3.

EXAMPLES OF DATA ANALYSIS

THE BEFORE-AND-AFTER DESIGN

The Before-and-after Design follows one group over time by taking measures both before and after exposure to an event. It is expected that the measure taken after the event will reflect some kind of improvement compared with before. Translated into numerical terms you will expect that the mean score obtained after exposure to the event will be significantly higher than the mean score obtained before the event. As an example the scores from the data set presented in table 5.4 will be compared. You will note that indeed a higher mean score was obtained after the event than before. Nonetheless you cannot accept the obtained difference in means at face value; you need to apply a test of *significant difference*.

Table 5.4 Reading scores of children aged 6–7 years before and after a teaching event

Pre-event	Post-event	Difference (pre-post)
4.5	7.8	3.3
4.7	4.6	–0.1
4.2	6.8	2.6
4.9	5.0	0.1
3.6	6.1	2.5
5.1	4.0	–1.1
3.8	4.7	0.9
30.8	39.0	8.2
4.4	5.6	1.2

By statistical significance is meant how much confidence you can have in your findings relative to what you might expect by chance. You need to be able to say that the probability of your result being obtained by chance is very slim: that despite errors of sampling your finding is systematic and due to something other than chance. To do this it is conventional to use what is termed the '**confidence limit**' of 5%. To say that a difference between means is statistically significant at the 5% level means that you can be confident that a value as large or larger than that obtained can only have occurred by chance 5 in 100 times. Following this rule you can be assured of making less than 5 errors in 100 decisions by concluding on the basis of the sample data that a '**true difference**' in means exists when in fact there is none – known as a Type I error of inference. The 5 % level of significance need not always be used: a higher or lower level of significance may be appropriate depending on how willing you are to make errors of inference. The lower the level of significance (e.g. 1% level or chance of error 1 in 100 times) the less chance there is of making a Type I error of inference. At the same time, however, you increase your chances of making a Type II error of inference – i.e. inferring that a difference is not reliable when in fact it is.

IDENTIFYING YOUR CONFIDENCE LIMITS

The confidence limit of 5% will vary in relation to two things: sample size and how well your predictions were specified. The smaller the sample size, the less room there is for scores to vary (i.e. the '**degrees of freedom**'). The threshold of the 5% confidence limit will decrease with increased sample size: the smaller the sample the bigger the effect you must obtain in order for it to reach significance. The threshold is also altered according to how precise you are in specifying the direction of the difference you expect to emerge. In gain score analysis the direction is already specified insofar as you expect only the group exposed to the event to exhibit an improvement. In this case, the confidence limit would be 'one-tailed' – i.e. it accounts for a difference in one particular direction. On occasion, however, it might not be clear which of two types of event will produce the bigger improvement. A difference in scores could arise in either direction. For example, you expect that two teaching events will differ in terms of the degree of performance improvement they will bring about but you are unsure which is the better. In this case the confidence limit is 'two-tailed' and will require a bigger effect in order for any differences obtained to be deemed significant. Taking you through a concrete example will make this notion of confidence limit much clearer.

The data in table 5.4 are derived from a group of seven school children who are exposed to a teaching event designed to improve their reading ability. Measures of their reading ability are taken before and after the event: i.e. the measurement process is repeated. Measurements obtained in this way are called **'related measures'** because they have been produced by the same set of people. This is relevant to your choice of statistical test. You need a test which is designed to identify systematic differences between the measures taken before and after the teaching event by comparing pairs of scores by the same individuals. The test recommended for this is known as the **'related t-test'**. The procedure for computing the related-t test is detailed in Greene & D'Oliveira (1982). Since you can expect 'gain' as a result of the teaching event the one-tailed criterion of confidence at the 5% level is used. The following two boxes provide examples of how data produced by other types of design might be handled.

ANALYSING THE DATA FROM A TIME-SERIES BEFORE-AND-AFTER DESIGN

Like the straightforward Before-and-after Design, the more complex time-series version requires 'repeated measurement': the test chosen should take account of the 'related' nature of the measurement. This design assumes that if the event of interest has been successful it will systematically interrupt any trends in the pattern of scores that might otherwise be obtained. So, we would expect a significantly greater gain in scores between time 3 and time 4 relative to that observed between time 1, 2 and 3 and between time 4, 5 and 6. One way to test this is to use a series of 'related t-tests' requiring multiple comparisons. The case study used in Chapter 3 involves an intervention designed to train careworkers working in a residential institution for violent children in 'control and restraint'. You will recall that the skill of ten care workers in handling instances of violence was independently observed and judged on a seven-point scale by two senior social workers at three-monthly intervals before and after the training intervention. At each time point, the ratings of each social worker for each care worker can be summed and averaged to produce a single score. The higher the score, the more skilled the care workers are judged to be in handling violence.

continued

continued –

	time 1	time 2	time 3	time 4	time 5	time 6
sum	27.5	30.0	33.0	58.0	61.0	64.0
mean	2.8	3.0	3.3	5.8	6.1	6.4

The actual compared with expected results are given below where under the expected (E) column 'nd' means 'no difference' and 'd' means 'difference'. The same notation is used under the actual (A) column.

	time 2		time 3		time 4		time 5		time 6	
	E	A	E	A	E	A	E	A	E	A
t1	nd	**nd**	nd	**nd**	d	**d**	d	**d**	d	**d**
t2	–		nd	**nd**	d	**d**	d	**d**	d	**d**
t3			–		d	**d**	d	**d**	d	**d**
t4					–		nd	**nd**	nd	**d**
t5							–		nd	**nd**

Simply by inspecting the means it is clear that a sharp improvement in care worker skill in handling instances of child violence is evident immediately after the training event and that this improvement is maintained. This suggests that the opportunity to consolidate and continue developing skills in handling instances of child violence after the training event facilitated some additional improvement. Might the care workers have improved anyway in time? One potential counter argument here might be that the benefit of training is to speed up the process of skill development.

ANALYSING THE DATA FROM A NOW-AND-THEN DESIGN

This example deals with data obtained from two (or more) groups of people, one of which has been exposed to an intervention of some kind whilst the other either has not or has been exposed to an alternative intervention. Using the example of young reoffenders described in Chapter 3 (page 40) it will be assumed that the data are in the form of frequencies (i.e. number of people in a particular category).

	Community	Institution	Row Totals
No reoffence	56	34	90
Reoffence	28	49	77
Column Total	84	83	**Grand Total** = 167

– continued

continued —

For this type of data a test of difference like the t-test or ANOVA is inappropriate. Instead a test is used that is specifically designed to handle frequency data, known as the **Chi-Square** (χ^2). This test requires a minimum of 20 people in the sample for it to work. Also, each person in the sample can only appear in one cell. It works by producing estimates of the number of people you can expect to fall into each category simply by chance and comparing these '**expected frequencies**' with the frequencies actually obtained. The '**obtained frequencies**' must be significantly different from the expected frequencies for the influence of chance to be ruled out. A significant χ^2 result, as in this example, will indicate whether overall there are differences in the pattern of reoffending according to whether intervention 1 or 2 is experienced. This might also be interpreted as an association between type of treatment and the likelihood of reoffending. To identify exactly where the differences lie means referring back to the differences obtained between expected and observed frequencies for each particular cell. The biggest differences arise for cell 1 (community/reoffending) and cell 3 (community/not reoffend) which means that a significant number of young males who undertook community service did not reoffend which is a finding that would not be expected by chance. This suggests that treatment of young offenders in the community has beneficial effects because the likelihood of reoffending is reduced relative to that associated with an institutional treatment. You can never be sure that the difference in type of treatment event 'explains' the findings since any number of additional factors could come into play. You would need to rule out an explanation in terms of age, social class, educational differences and so on.

HOW TO INTERPRET THE FINDINGS

The *t*-test result was not significant using the 5% criterion of confidence. This shows that the improvement in reading ability demonstrated by the children could have been produced by chance alone. On the basis of the difference in means it would be tempting to conclude that the teaching event worked but a more stringent test of the differences between means suggests otherwise. The findings can be explained by wide individual differences in the patterns of change observed. Just by inspecting column three in table 5.4 it becomes clear that although some children demonstrated an improvement in their reading ability others did not; in fact, one appeared to become worse. The pattern of variation in the changes observed therefore is not very systematic. Any number of factors other than the teaching event could explain it. For example, some children may have demonstrated improvement because the teaching strategy suited their learning style whilst not being of much additional help to others. The child who performed much worse at post-event may have been experiencing a lot of test anxiety. All you can do is speculate. Inferential tests like the *t*-test will treat this kind of variation as sampling error. The more the error – especially in the scores obtained from such a small sample of people – the less confident you can be about the effect of a particular event.

The above point alludes to the difference between the statistical and the practical significance of a finding. The former is a neutral indicator of probability whilst the latter refers to an interpretation of the findings in relation to a) a conceptual model or set of assumptions which provide the rationale for the event of interest and/or b) their real-life implications. A result can be statistically significant but not very meaningful at the practical level. Let's say that a psychotropic drug administered for depression is found to have deleterious behavioural side-effects at a probability level of 5 in 100 (i.e. the 5% level of significance); in other words, one in 20 people administered the drug is likely to develop these side-effects. Would you administer or take this drug? The statistic is neutral and requires interpretation.

Returning to the example of a teaching event you could argue that since three out of seven children (i.e. almost 43%) showed substantial improvement in their reading ability it would be unfortunate simply to conclude that the teaching event did not work since clearly it did in some cases. Indeed, if you are pushed to demonstrate that the event did have some effect you might decide to reduce the confidence level of your test to the 10% level in which case the obtained value of t would then be statistically significant! Alternatively you might refer to this as indicative of a 'trend'. Before considering the implications of this it is worth while considering why an effect might not be (very) statistically significant:

- the prediction could be wrong
- the theory or intervention model might be unsound
- the measures used to test an effect may be unreliable or invalid
- the design was faulty, i.e. e.g. lack of control over the intervention or inappropriate design
- inadequate sample, or sampling bias
- some or all of these in combination.

If, on speculating about the reasons why some children improved and others did not, you decide that the event may have beneficial effects only under certain conditions, you may decide to conduct some additional analyses. You may note from table 5.4 that those who showed the most improvement obtained some of the lowest reading scores to begin with whilst those who showed little or no improvement (or who got a lower score afterwards) obtained the highest score to begin with. This might suggest some kind of 'interaction effect': the teaching event leads to improvement only in those whose initial reading ability is lower than average. Omitting these kinds of things from consideration can lead to inadequate sampling and inappropriate predictions. In itself this might be the angle you choose to take when presenting the findings.

BEFORE-AND-AFTER DESIGN WITH CONTROLS

This type of design is probably the most complex to analyse especially if it involves more than two groups. To keep things simple an example involving only two groups will be used. Two sixth form classes of adolescents (aged 16 to 17 years) matched in socio-economic status are involved in a six-month study on safer sex. Three months after completing an inventory of sexual attitudes and behaviours, one class of adolescents is involved in a workshop designed to facilitate safer sexual practices. The other class is not exposed to any intervention event. Three months later both classes of adolescents complete the inventory again.

This design combines two components: a 'repeated measure' component and an 'independent' component. The **repeated measure component** is that members of each class provide two lots of data (i.e. using the same measures) – one lot before and the other lot after one of the classes was exposed to the intervention. The **independent component** is that two different classes of people are being compared. This mixed character of the design is crucial to your choice of statistical test and to the soundness of the conclusion that can be drawn about the value of the intervention.

The pre-event testing provides an important control since each class of adolescents may have started at different levels on the measures of interest. Once any discrepancy in starting points is accounted for, any systematic departures from this can, in theory, be attributed to the effect of the event. The statistic you choose to analyse the data you obtain must take into account both variation in 'starting points' and variation between and within each class of adolescents in any changes that occur over time. It should be able to tell you that despite variation in starting points, the class exposed to the event exhibit a systematic gain over time relative to that of the class not exposed to the event (known as a 'main effect' or systematic influence of one variable on another). Specifically, you expect adolescents exposed to the workshop event to be significantly more likely to practise safer sex afterwards than before it, whilst no changes are expected amongst those who were not exposed to the workshop event.

The table below presents a summary of the data for this evaluation exercise. The scores range from 1 to 7; the higher the score the more likely it is that 'safer' sex is being practised. To keep things relatively simple, there are only ten adolescents in each class.

Table 5.5 Mean 'Sexual practice' scores of adolescents 16–17 years (sd)

	Pre-event test	Post-event test
Class 1 (treatment)	2.5 (0.81)	5.3 (1.01)
Class 2 (no treatment)	2.4 (0.92)	2.0 (0.63)

From this it is noted that there is little discrepancy between the treatment and comparison groups in their starting points on the measure of interest. Adolescents in both classes are generally unlikely to practice 'safer sex'. The amount of variation within each class is also similar. After being involved in the workshop event, Class 1 exhibits a large 'gain' in scores (mean difference = +2.8) relative to Class 2 who were not involved in the workshop event. Class 2 in fact exhibit slightly 'lower' scores (mean difference = –0.4) at the end of the six-month period of the study. You might be tempted to accept these results at face value. However, although the gain of Class 1 is indeed substantial relative to that of Class 2 there is much more class variation than before (standard deviation = 1.01 versus standard deviation = 0.81). A statistical test will account for these changes in variation as well as in the mean scores. Moreover, if you can demonstrate the statistical significance of your results it will add substance and credibility to your claims for the benefits of the event in question.

To do this a test is needed which is one of a family of tests designed to apportion out, control for and explain subtle variation in the data known as the 'Analysis of Variance' (ANOVA) for the

Mixed 2-Factor Design. CLASS comprises one of the factors (remember this is the independent component) which has two levels (Class 1 and Class 2) and TIME comprises the other factor (the repeated measures component) which also has two levels: pre-test and post-test. The procedure for computing this analysis is detailed in Greene and D'Oliveira (1982) using a simple step-by-step guide. The results from the analysis are presented in the conventional form, however, to provide guidelines for the process of interpretation.

First, clarify your predictions. The Mixed 2-factor Design ANOVA test will identify systematic variation originating from differences between CLASS of adolescents in the form of a **main effect** (see page 93). Likewise any systematic variation due to changes over TIME will be identified also in the form of a main effect (ibid.). Of interest here is what is known as the 'interaction effect' originating from variation in the patterns of changes exhibited by each particular CLASS over TIME. Since Class 1 is expected to exhibit change whilst Class 2 is not (taking into consideration their starting points) you are looking for the interaction effect to be statistically significant. Neither a strong TIME or CLASS main effect is expected since you would hope a) that there was little difference between CLASSES other than those induced by the intervention and b) that any positive

Table 5.6 ANOVA results for the 'safer sex' intervention using the Mixed 2-Factor Design

Source of variation	df	SS	MS	F ratio
Between-Subjects	1	47.9		
CLASS	1	28.9	28.9	3.0 df=1,39 ns
Group/Error	2	19.0	9.5	
Within-Subjects		50.0		
TIME	1	14.4	14.4	2.9 df=1,39 ns
GROUP x TIME	1	25.6	25.6	5.1 df=1,39 p<0.05
GxT/Error	2	10.0	5.0	
Total SS	39	97.9		

Key
df   = degrees of freedom
SS   = sum of squares
MS   = mean of sum of squares
F ratio = the statistical effect tested by the procedure
ns   = not significant
G   = group
T   = time

changes observed are confined to the class which received the intervention. From the table opposite it can be seen that the results confirm these expectations.

Neither the main effect for CLASS nor for TIME is statistically significant (ns) whereas the interaction between CLASS and TIME is significant at the 5% level ($p<0.05$). From the pattern of means in table 5.5 you know that it is Class 1 which exhibits significant change over time relative to Class 2. There is only a one in 20 chance of this change being due to sampling error. You can conclude therefore that the workshop event successfully facilitated 'safer' sexual practices amongst the 16 to 17 year-old adolescents who received it.

Sceptics may provide alternative explanations in terms of design faults. For example, it might be argued that simply by repeating the test the adolescents involved will have become more alert to the issues and this may induce change in itself. In the current example, both classes received the same inventory of sexual attitudes and behaviour at pre- and post-event testing so both will have been 'sensitised' to the issue of 'safer sex'. Yet Class 2 were less likely to practise safer sex after completing both tests than before.

Another common criticism stems from the reliance of events of the kind described here on volunteers. If both the treatment and comparison group contain volunteers then the effect of the event itself can be partialled out easily. The only problem would be one of not being able to generalize the implications of the findings to the population of non-volunteers. If just the treatment group is comprised of volunteers then factors associated with self-selection in themselves – for example, being concerned about the issue of safer sex, already practising safer sex, or simply 'ready' for the intervention – may determine the outcomes obtained, quite apart from the effect of the workshop event. So long as you can show that adolescents in each class are equivalent in terms of their relationship with the study (e.g. all had obtained parental consent) then the findings are unlikely to be contaminated by class differences in their motivation to be involved.

A weakness of the present analysis is that it does not provide answers to the question of how or why the workshop event had the effect it did. Ways in which the analyses might be extended to include these kinds of considerations are discussed later on.

THE ISSUES OF PREDICTION AND EXPLANATION

Some evaluations may be designed to answer questions about processes and how these relate to certain outcomes. For example, you might want to know why departments within an organization which have a policy of employee participation are more successful in facilitating job commitment than those which do not. One way to find out is to unravel the implications of the policy of employee participation in terms of concrete practices and procedures (e.g. management style and practices, work patterns, job characteristics, work environment etc.) to identify variables which might be associated with the outcome obtained. These various **process factors** can then be systematically correlated (using the coefficient of correlation) with the outcome to examine the character and strength of the relationship.

The coefficient of correlation can vary between a perfect positive correlation of +1.0 (a high score on one measure is accompanied by the likelihood of a high score on the other) to a perfect negative correlation of –1.0 (a high score on one measure is accompanied by a low score on the other). Most correlations are less than 1.0 in which case there will always be some errors of prediction.

The coefficient of correlation is limited, however, to an expression of the degree to which two factors covary. It does not allow inferences to be made about what causes what. If, for example, we find that democratic management style 'predicts' (i.e. co-varies with) employee commitment, we cannot assume that one is the cause of the other. Some other hidden or parallel influences may be at play (e.g. team spirit).

One way to overcome this problem is to employ multivariate forms of data handling (such as regression analysis or path analysis) which have the power to estimate the relative power of a number of factors (i.e. multiple variables) to explain variation in the outcome of interest simultaneously. This is not, however, the place to provide details on how to select and use these more sophisticated tools. All of them rely on computer-based forms of data handling. The interested reader is advised to consult the more specialist texts listed in the references at the end of the book.

The task for now is to help you think about how to handle your data by identifying exactly what you need it to tell you. The figure below provides a simple decision tree to help you identify which type of test you might use.

Figure 5.1 Decision Tree for Test Selection

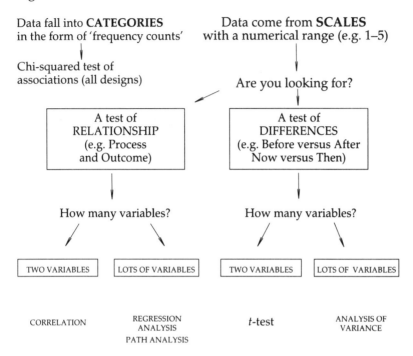

Data fall into **CATEGORIES**
in the form of 'frequency counts'

Chi-squared test of
associations (all designs)

Data come from **SCALES**
with a numerical range (e.g. 1–5)

Are you looking for?

A test of
RELATIONSHIP
(e.g. Process
and Outcome)

A test of
DIFFERENCES
(e.g. Before versus After
Now versus Then)

How many variables?

How many variables?

TWO VARIABLES   LOTS OF VARIABLES   TWO VARIABLES   LOTS OF VARIABLES

CORRELATION   REGRESSION
ANALYSIS
PATH ANALYSIS

t-test

ANALYSIS OF
VARIANCE

Chapter Six

Presenting the Findings

Knowing how to analyse evaluation data is the key to translating information into intelligence but this must be complemented by the ability to present any findings in a suitable way for each particular target audience. Findings may be required either in report form or in oral form. In some instances, it may be up to the evaluator to decide how best to present them (including the option of disseminating findings in an interactive and informal way, e.g. in project team meetings or task force workshops). This chapter advises on various ways of presenting evaluation findings. In particular, practical suggestions are made for presenting information persuasively, for handling a range of audience reactions and for overcoming organizational inertia in the face of recommendations for change.

PREPARING TO DISSEMINATE EVALUATION INFORMATION

Preparation is essential. It involves a number of considerations.

CLARIFY THE OBJECTIVES

For example, your evaluation may have been conducted to provide a needs assessment, to describe an intervention programme, to report findings, to draw conclusions, to make recommendations for change, or all of these.

TAILOR THE INFORMATION TO AUDIENCE INTERESTS

You should consider any needs, concerns or fears that your audience may have. Whilst various steps can be taken during the conduct of the evaluation to pre-empt any 'ripple effects' (i.e. objections, hostilities and 'inertias' – i.e. unwillingness to participate) that can be engendered, any outstanding concerns will need to be dealt with at the presentation stage. Moreover, if the findings are such that recommendations for change need to be made, this will foster its own nexus of 'ripples'. For instance, an evaluation of care worker behaviour might demonstrate clearly that certain ways of handling children with special learning difficulties are inappropriate. (For example, a forceful/reprimanding style of care may be associated with an aggressive or withdrawing reaction in the child.) But such findings are, of course, likely to arouse emotion. Being able to anticipate reactions of this kind is the first step to dealing with them.

FOCUS THE DISSEMINATION

Your objective provides a firm guide as to what should go into the presentation – ensuring focus and incisiveness throughout. The good presenter delivers only what is absolutely necessary to achieve the end in mind. Evaluation can yield information that can be used to validate or condemn existing practices as well as providing pointers to improvement. Inevitably, the conclusions drawn and the recommendations made are derived from an interpretation of the findings and are therefore open to contest. All conclusions and recommendations must be well substantiated.

IDENTIFY THE MEDIUM FOR DISSEMINATION

The terms of reference guiding the evaluation exercise may stipulate the precise form in which the findings are presented. Both written and oral forms of presentation may be required, addressed perhaps to different audiences and therefore guided by different objectives. In choosing an appropriate forum, one of the determining factors might be the particular relationship that the evaluator has with those involved. If the relationship is participatory the evaluator may be obliged to present brief interim reports in verbal or written form to a small number of interested parties (e.g. at committee or board meetings). If the relationship is non-participatory the evaluator may be required to present the information in a lengthier, more 'official' type of document or at more formal public venues to a mixed audience. Choice of media makes all the difference when it comes to presenting sensitive material, i.e. material that invalidates or condemns current practices.

ANALYSING THE TARGET AUDIENCE

- Who needs to know and exactly why? Who are the key decision-makers and by when do they need certain information?
- How detailed is their knowledge of the evaluation project?
- What kind of opinions do they have of the evaluation project? (For example, do they have a particular axe to grind?)
- What kind of opinions do they have about you and your department/organization?
- What reasons might they have for attending/reading the presentation/report?
- What advantages will result from the evaluation project *to them*?
- What disadvantages will result *to them*?
- What is their composition?
  - age group
  - male/female
  - vocabulary understanding level
  - expertise/status
  - education level.
- What are the important issues for them?
  - their beliefs
  - their feelings
  - their values.
- What kind of presentation/reporting techniques are likely to engender a negative reaction?
- How might you handle or overcome their objections?
- What strategies might you use to help the audience identify what's in the project for them?
- How interested are they likely to be in the fine details of the project relative to the overall picture?
- Is the audience likely to be turned off by statistical analysis or will this add credibility to what you say?
- Is the audience likely to be turned off by anecdotes or will these enrich or add clarity to what you say?

DECIDE EXACTLY WHAT YOU NEED TO SAY

To ensure selectivity in presenting the findings you will need to answer the following questions:
- What exactly does the audience/reader need to *know?*
- What exactly will the audience/reader need to *do?*
- What exactly will *I* need to *demonstrate?*

CATEGORIZE THE INFORMATION SELECTED

Once the key bits of information have been identified they can be categorized into meaningful sections or blocks and then organized in a sequence that will make sense to the audience, in keeping with the objective(s) of the presentation.

STRUCTURE FOR CLARITY AND CONTROL

Structure provides the framework for the delivery of information. It helps the listener or reader to make sense of what is said and to keep track of this. The conventional way to provide structure is to follow the old adage:

- Tell them what you are going to tell them   *Introduction*
- Tell them   *Main body*
- Tell them what you have told them   *Summary.*

BREAK UP THE INFORMATION INTO MANAGEABLE PARTS

In a long presentation, the main points can get lost in the breadth of coverage or depth of detail. The main body of the presentation should be organized into sections, perhaps even subsections, and each treated as a self-contained unit. Each section/subsection must be briefly introduced and at the end a summary of points should be provided before moving on to the next section. For an oral presentation, this may imply a rigid structure. However, structure can be provided in a conversational way, e.g. 'During this section I will . . .' and 'To recap . . . .'. Conversational devices can also be used to signal transition from one section to another: 'In this section I have dealt with . . . ..in the next section I will show you . . . ' In this way, links can be forged between sections in a way that maintains the flow of the presentation.

Visual support can also be employed at the summary stage. For example, key words can be highlighted on the overhead projector. Reiteration of the main points at the end of each section will reinforce the presentation and thus help people to remember them.

SEQUENCE THE INFORMATION PERSUASIVELY

❑ Build up the arguments progressively by demonstrating that:

- the study was necessary
- the way it was conducted was the 'best' for the task
- the findings are sound
- the recommendations meet given needs and concerns, i.e. there are pay-offs.

❑ Tailor the arguments to the specific issues of concern. Standard arguments rarely work unless they address the concerns by chance. The audience (or readers) must be able to make sense of the findings within their own frame of reference. For example, there is no point in providing cost-benefit statistics if people are more concerned with the project ethics. This makes a distinction between the *nature* of the intervention and the *design* of the intervention. It also places demands on your ability to put yourself in others' shoes.

❑ Separate facts from opinions about those facts. Facts are less easily contested (so long as the methods used to obtain them are sound) whereas conclusions and recommendations are open to dispute. Conclusions must be closely tied to the facts to minimize any degree of doubt that they raise; this should ensure overall that recommendations are perceived to be a logical consequence of the facts.

CASE STUDY: A PLANNING EXERCISE

EXERCISE 4

A social worker has just completed a programme of observations of the behaviours of care workers and children in two local authority day nurseries for children with special learning difficulties. The nurseries are matched in all their characteristics except for the ratio of staff to children. Your objective is to provide a progress report to the local authority Research Committee who are coordinating and funding the project, and also to debrief the care workers in each of the two participating nurseries.

The social worker encounters some hostility in one of the day nurseries: care workers were obviously uncomfortable with her presence and kept asking questions. In some cases she found it difficult if not impossible to obtain adequate 'samples' of behaviour across all of the situations required by the schedule because of the lack of staff co-operation. Moreover, in this nursery – which is the one with the lower care worker-to-child ratio – what she found was fairly negative.

The following is a record of the social worker's observations. It documents the frequency of occurrence of certain staff behaviours (out of a total of 100 instances of behaviour) in each of the nurseries. (But note that a more fine-grained analysis is yet to be performed.)

	Day Nursery 1 Staff ratio 1:3	Day Nursery 2 Staff ratio 1:1
Care Worker Behaviours		
Supporting	40	31
Encouraging/inviting	25	63
Reprimanding	10	2
Criticizing	15	2
Forceful	10	2

➤ For each of the audiences the social worker is to address, through what medium (oral/written) would you choose to report on your progress (and debrief the care workers) and why?

➤ In the medium you have chosen for each particular audience, how would you present the findings and why?

➤ What potential problems might you encounter in presenting these findings as they stand?

Pitfalls to avoid when debriefing the staff:
Day nursery care workers are likely to be defensive, especially if they have been obliged to participate without knowing what the

continued

continued –

study is about. They may fear the implications of the study for their job security and will need to be reassured. When debriefing the staff, there are a number of potential pitfalls to avoid:

- Presenting the findings without providing a rationale for the evaluation and the methods used. Effectively it is concerned with identifying the influence of certain organizational factors (care worker–child ratio) on care workers' behaviours rather than staff performance *per se*. Far from pointing the finger at the individual care worker, the findings should yield implications for change only at the organizational level (e.g. increased resources).

- Presenting the findings in an over-generalized and/or judgemental way. For example: 'Day nursery 2 is substantially better than Day nursery 1 in its care of children with learning difficulties'. This will exacerbate hostilities and, anyway, has nothing to do with what the evaluation was really about.

- Presenting the findings without providing them with an interpretation of a) the observation categories and b) the pattern of numbers and what they imply.

- Presenting the findings out of context. For example, providing them with counts of frequency of occurrence of certain behaviours as if no account has been taken of the context of their occurrence and/or as if staff are 'inherently' bad at caring for children with special learning difficulties.

- Presenting only one set of findings. For example, focusing on the care workers' behaviours without identifying the relationship they have either to the context of their occurrence (initiating factors) or their outcomes (how the child responds).

- Presenting the findings in a form which a) is inaccessible to staff (i.e. too daunting to read or just too technical), and b) where they have no opportunity to ask questions about or to respond to what is said.

- Debriefing the care workers in a public forum – i.e. care workers from both day nurseries together. This could give rise to unnecessary friction and would constitute public humiliation for staff from the day nursery whose behaviour is less appropriate to the care of children with special learning difficulties - even though this might be traceable to inadequate resourcing.

Pitfalls to avoid when providing a progress report to the Research Committee:

- Confusing the facts with the interpretation of those facts.

– - *continued*

continued –

> Neither the evaluation, nor the findings warrant definitive statements being made about the influence of 'care worker–child ratio' on care worker behaviour and in turn, the behaviour of the child. Only two day nurseries are involved. Even though they were matched in all but the care worker–child ratio there may be some other unidentified factor involved which can account for the findings.
>
> - Drawing conclusions without a full and thorough consideration of the evidence and any alternative explanations for the findings.
> - Being overselective in presenting the findings and the context of the findings.
> - Providing premature 'answers' because of the emphasis on getting results.
> - Downplaying the weaknesses of the study or difficulties encountered in conducting the study because of a need to demonstrate 'progress': it may be that you need to extend the study to include other day nurseries and/or to tap into other sources of evidence (e.g. by conducting interviews with the care workers, or profiling the characteristics of each day nursery to identify similarities/differences between them).

DIFFERENCES BETWEEN WRITTEN AND ORAL PRESENTATION

In both written and oral form an evaluation presentation aims to disseminate the results of an investigation or to outline the facts of an event on the basis of which decisions can be made and action taken. An evaluation presentation is designed to make something happen – it must result in action. Although similar in their overall aims, both written and oral presentation require a particular type of communication. Some of the distinguishing characteristics are summarized below.

COMPARISON OF WRITTEN AND ORAL PRESENTATION	
Oral	*Written*
- Limited coverage within the time available. - Emphasis on the personal skills and style of the presenter.	- Potentially no limit on breadth/depth of coverage. - Relatively depersonalized medium of emphasis on the presentation.

continued

continued —

Oral	Written
• In-built flexibility. It can be responsive to audience reactions.	• Inflexible/non-interactive – relies completely on having anticipated audience needs and concerns.
• It requires some 'thinking on your feet'.	• Everything can be planned in.
• The presenter can 'lose' people easily.	• Opportunity for the reader to re-read and digest the report.
• It can gain the attention and interest of those who might not otherwise choose to read a report.	• It can alienate the reader's interest with too many facts and figures or technical details.
• Visual aids can be used to structure and pace the presentation.	• Tables and graphics can be incorporated in the presentation.
• A conversational style of language is possible.	• Requires greater attention to written structure and grammatical correctness.
• Potentially more control over interpretation of findings.	• Potentially less control over the interpretaion of findings since people have more time to digest the facts and consider alternatives.
• This tends to be planned at the later stages.	• It can be written up bit by bit as the project progresses and as information comes to light.

WEAKNESSES OF WRITTEN OR ORAL PRESENTATIONS

Written forms – potential weaknesses
Executive summary
A condensed overview of the project findings risks being taken out of context due to:
• the absence of important background information
• the lack of opportunity to trace the logic behind the design used, the conclusions drawn and the recommendations made
• the definitive style in which the executive summary is written, which can engender an illusion of the findings being more clear cut than they actually are.

— - *continued*

continued –

The interim progress report
- This can inadvertently overplay the problems, difficulties and constraints being faced.
- It risks confusing or alienating the reader from the whole picture.

The final report
- A report addressed to different audiences cannot address all their needs and concerns without the report becoming unwieldy or ill-focused.

Oral forms – potential weaknesses

The quick oral report
- This challenges the skills of the presenter in providing a balanced but brief and succinct overview of progress so far.
- Limited scope for the use of visual aids or other types of presentation support.
- It projects the credibility of the presenter into the spotlight in a more intense way than the formal presentation.
- There is a risk of overgeneralizing or presenting the findings in an oversimplified way because of time pressure and the need to be definitive.

The formal presentation
- This relies on a thorough analysis of audience needs and concerns.
- It tends to get bogged down with detail or too many facts and figures.
- There is little opportunity to monitor and respond to audience reactions other than at the end.
- Too many visual aids can clutter the presentation or be used as a smokescreen.
- It is tempting to 'read' the presentation from a verbatim script.

The informal presentation
- The possibility of audience involvement can prove disruptive to the structure and flow of the presentation. The presenter must be able to maintain composure in the face of hostile or defensive questioning, objections and other reactions.
- It challenges the persuasive ability of the presenter.

MANAGING THE DELIVERY OF AN ORAL PRESENTATION

IDENTIFYING THE VENUE AND SCHEDULING THE PRESENTATION

The choice of venue is an important planning consideration: it will influence the style of the presentation and the kind of atmosphere engendered. A presentation addressed to a small number of committee members demands quite a different style than one addressed to a very mixed audience in a large public forum. Audience involvement and discussion is possible in the former but is hardly feasible in the latter. On the other hand the formal atmosphere of a boardroom adds a different flavour to the presentation than the relative informality of a public forum.

THINKING ON YOUR FEET

The ability to think on one's feet makes the difference between a good and an excellent presentation. Some room for manoeuvre can be structured into the session but there is always the occasion where something unanticipated occurs. For example, you can anticipate the types of questions that might be asked and how they might be dealt with but then find that an awkward or difficult question is asked or reactions are more negative than you had foreseen.

CONTROL – THE KEY TO AN EFFECTIVE PRESENTATION

The feeling of being in control (i.e. confidence in the subject matter, thorough preparation and perception that you are equipped with the necessary skills) will help minimize anxiety as well as increase the likelihood of success. Three key aspects of control can be identified, each of which requires systematic attention:

- Control of *strategy* – how the presentation is delivered.

- Control of *substance* – what the presentation is about.

- Control of *personal style* – the particular way the presentation is managed: e.g. managing personal credibility or gaining audience rapport.

Strategy and substance are interrelated. For example, the politically sensitive nature of evaluation makes it especially important a) to anticipate the kinds of reactions that might be invoked and b) to build strategies for managing these reactions into the structure of the presentation. In turn, the issues dealt with, and the information delivered, will depend directly on what needs to be achieved.

MANAGING AUDIENCE INVOLVEMENT

The more opportunity provided for audience involvement the more likely it is that their commitment to the evaluation and its outcomes will be gained. At the very least, this may take the form of a question-and-answer session at the end of the presentation. In the case of imposed non-participatory evaluation the scope for this may be limited. At most, a structured discussion may be possible but this will depend very much on the size of the audience, the type of venue, how much time there is and the degree of formality required.

MANAGING ATTENTION

Without paying attention, your audience will not absorb what is said, let alone remember or accept it. If their motivation is high, attention is also likely to be high. However, there are limits to the amount of attention that any group of people, no matter how sophisticated they are, will be able to maintain throughout a presentation, whatever kind it is. Since attention span is limited it needs to be actively managed. The senses through which information is assimilated (i.e. mainly through listening in an oral presentation) tire easily. The amount of information an individual takes in will be maximized by ensuring plenty of variation and also by helping the audience to make sense of what you say. Variation in verbal presentation can be derived from:

- the use of visual aids

- gesticulation and varied expression (verbal and non-verbal)

- using eye-contact to engender rapport

- the use of video or audiotape

- the use of questions

- discussion, and/or involving others in some way

- the use of pace, tone, volume and silence

- the use of humour.

HELPING MAKE SENSE OF INFORMATION

Packaging the information into meaningful categories, e.g. theme by theme, helps the listener to absorb and remember. Structuring the categories in some kind of sequence provides memorable signposts. For example, in an order that coincides with the steps involved in a process of programme implementation. Other ways in which meaning can be ensured are as follows:

- Relate new 'abstract' ideas or concepts to the concrete and familiar e.g. by association (metaphor, analogy, examples).

- Provide concrete examples whenever possible.

- Use graphics to explain something complex or hard to understand.

- Use tables and/or figures to illustrate trends, changes or relationships.

- Provide intermittent summaries to reinforce the main points.

STRUCTURING THE FORMAL PRESENTATION

Introduction
Who you are and *where* you are from
- to help manage personal credibility
- to forge links with previous presentations.

Aim and *agenda* of the presentation
- indicate the intended outcomes
- make the structure explicit
- indicate any back-up material you can provide.

Benefits and *pay-offs* for the audience
- explain why it is worth listening
- dispel any false expectations
- indicate the pay-offs they can expect.

Time
- indicate how long the presentation will take.

Main Body
Project context – which describes how the evaluation programme was initiated and why, its aims, how many people were involved, what particular groups of people and why (i.e. their composition,

continued

continued —

on what basis they were selected), links between the programme and any needs assessment that was conducted, legal or policy requirements or any other mandates underlying the programme objectives. The degree of detail included here depends on the needs and concerns of the audience and the objective of the report (it may not be safe to assume that they know all the ins and outs of the project).

Description of the study – the design, methodology and materials/ instruments/procedures/activities/resources used in the project are described and explained (i.e. what, why and how they were used). The context of the implementation is also described. For example: Did some of the participants drop out and, if so, why? Who was involved in implementing the project? On what basis were they selected and what qualifications were required (or training)? Were there any problems encountered during the implementation phase and, if so, what effect did they have? Again, the amount of detail will depend on the presentation objectives.

Results – describes the way the information was handled and records the results of this. You may also need to consider the implications on the results of people dropping out of the programme on the results.

Discussion – interpretation of the findings, conclusions and recommendations. Costs and benefits of the programme.

Ending the Presentation
A summary of the main points (i.e. the facts, your interpretation of the facts in the conclusions drawn, and the recommendations being made). You may prefer to leave the conclusions and recommendations until this stage, in which case a summary of the main findings will need to be presented first. A discussion or question-and-answer session can be included here along with any supporting documentation.

MANAGING MOTIVATION

One cannot guarantee that an audience is uniformly motivated to hear what needs to be said. Some people may be motivated to undermine publicly the credibility of the project or to reconstrue certain findings to suit their own specific ends. Such blocks to the success of a presentation (and indeed the entire project) cannot be dealt with in any easy way. However, to a certain extent one can temper any initial scepticism or negativity by:

- Providing people with good reasons to listen (irrespective of whether they agree or not with what has happened so far). The pay-offs outlined must make sense to the audience in that they can relate genuinely to them.

- Acknowledging rather than ignoring scepticism to encourage people to feel that at least their needs and concerns are being noted.

- Establishing a norm of involvement early on by indicating to the audience when they may ask questions – i.e. throughout, early on, or at the end of the presentation – or by actively inviting questions.

- Encouraging the audience to think about the findings. For example, they may be asked to suggest ways in which the findings might be interpreted, to consider what kind of conclusions they would draw and/or to make any recommendations.

- Inviting the audience to express how they feel about the evaluation and accept what they say at face value rather than try to discount it.

- Using a form of words that the audience can identify with, thus ensuring that conclusions and recommendations are perceived as credible and useful. The same outline can be phrased in a different way depending on the audience.

One may be wary of encouraging involvement for fear of releasing hostile reactions or of not being able to handle audience objections. Yet members of the audience may resent the lack of opportunity to express their point of view, which can make it difficult for the presenter to make any recommendations for change. Negative feelings and objections do not disappear on their own.

Audience attention and audience motivation are interrelated: if the audience lacks motivation their attention is unlikely to be guaranteed unless they have a particular axe to grind (in which case they may attend only very selectively, i.e. to suit their own agenda). Likewise, if attention wanes – because the presentation is inappropriately pitched or difficult to understand – the audience may also lose motivation.

QUESTIONS, OBJECTIONS AND HOSTILE REACTIONS

❑ A silent reaction to a presentation is unhealthy: silence does not necessarily mean acceptance. Issues and concerns left unaddressed will crop up later on as barriers to the implementation of change. The more explicit the reactions of the audience the easier it will be to address them.

❑ Anticipate salient issues and concerns and tailor the presentation accordingly.

❑ Monitor audience reactions, both verbal (e.g. types of objections, questions and comments) and non-verbal (e.g. facial expressions or extent of engagement) and deal with them in a direct and focused way.

— *MAKING AN EFFECTIVE PRESENTATION* —

EXERCISE 5

Think of a presentation you have attended which in your eyes was very poor and contrast this with one you have attended which was excellent or very good. Think back and try to identify exactly what it was that led you to characterize each one either as poor or good. Write these points down and, where possible, think about what the presenter did or did not do that was bad or good.

The poor presentation   *The good presentation*

....
....
....
....
....
....

Identify the skills you think are important to a good presentation:

....
....
....
....
....
....
....

❑ Substantiate opinions with evidence. Invite sceptics amongst the audience to offer their own interpretations of the evidence.

❑ Avoid bluffing in response to questions that are difficult to answer. Maintain professional credibility by offering suggestions as to where or how an answer may be found.

❑ Play back audience objections by seeking clarification of the issues which underly them to demonstrate genuine concern with understanding their needs and anxieties. This will enhance trust.

❑ Acknowledge any negative feelings conveyed. For example, 'I can see that you are unhappy with the implications of these findings . . .'. Avoid meaningless platitudes or the negation of feelings, such as 'There is no need to worry . . .' or 'Your anger is unfounded since . . . '. These tend to exacerbate rather than defuse strong feelings. Ask questions which will help pinpoint the reasons for the feelings expressed and then address them. For example, 'The recommendations I am making are quite a shock to you and I can see that many of you are feeling quite angry. What is it exactly that you don't like about them?'

❑ Beware of domination by one or two members or sections of the audience: involve others as much as possible. Those with positive views may be able to help argue a case.

WHAT TO AVOID DURING A PRESENTATION

- Reading a report verbatim – this can be stilted or read in monotone, sometimes too fast, and it can reduce eye contact undermining rapport with audience.

- Bluffing your way through an argument with irrelevant waffle for the sake of an answer.

- Being overly technical and full of alienating jargon.

- Tendency to hide behind too many visual aids and thereby to swamp the audience, or confuse and destroy the basis of an argument.

- Padding out the talk with unnecessary or irrelevant information.

-continued

continued —

- Resist making too many jokes; this can undermine the importance of a message.

- Avoid excessive use of abstractions and metaphors.

- Talking down to an audience.

- Making people feel foolish when answering their questions.

- Forming factual statements out of opinions or not backing up opinions with facts.

- Arousing defence and hostility by being judgemental, adopting an air of superiority, a dogmatic attitude, apathy and disinterest, or making unwarranted assumptions.

WRITING THE REPORT

CHECKLIST FOR ORGANIZING WRITTEN MATERIAL

- Identify the relevant information for inclusion, ensuring that all items are essential rather than 'nice to know'.

- Establish the framework of the report including the sections, sub-sections and their headings. Indicate under which heading each piece of material will be included. Arrange the information in note form.

- Check the order of the sections and sub-sections. Does the order make sense? Do each of the sections piece together in a way that ensures that the writing of the report will flow easily? Does each section contribute to the objective?

- Select a title that reflects the purpose of the report but which is short and punchy.

- Draw conclusions and recommendations consistent with the facts. Decide whether to group them in a section of their own or to distribute them among the various sections to which they most closely relate.

- Organize the appendices. These enable details to be included but in a less distracting form than amidst the text of the report. Too many details can sometimes interrupt the thread of thought.

OUTLINE STRUCTURE FOR AN EVALUATION REPORT

Title page
- title
- title of programme, programme location and duration
- identification (author, department/organization, date)
- circulation (a list of those who will receive the report).

List of contents (in a report of six pages or more)
- headings and sub-headings
- index of tables and figures (in a longer report).

Summary of the whole report to provide a complete overview.

Introduction
- terms of reference/statement of purpose
- project history and context
- description of other similar studies that have been done.

Elaboration
- procedure
    project design
    method of selecting participants and assigning them
       to groups
    participant characteristics
    project activities
    project tools/instruments/measures
    project implementation: by whom, their qualifications
       and training
- results
- conclusions
- recommendations.

Reiteration
- summary of findings
- summary of conclusions
- summary of recommendations.

References and sources

Appendices and glossary of terms

- Structure the report. Often firm in-house guidelines are available on how to structure a report. A typical evaluation report will adhere to the structure characterized in the box opposite.

DETERMINING THE DEGREE OF DETAIL REQUIRED

If the report is to be a lasting record details may be needed on the background and context of the programme. This can be written at the planning stage when information is freshly acquired. It will help ensure that a clear grasp of the context is attained.

ENSURING THE CREDIBILITY OF CONCLUSIONS AND RECOMMENDATIONS

The section on conclusions and recommendations is probably the most significant component of an evaluation report. Conclusions should be 'credible' given the facts and in light of the readers' needs and concerns:

- Summarize the findings and any inferences that you have generated from them so that readers are able to trace the logic you have used in producing recommendations.

- Emphasize the practical significance of the recommendations and indicate the benefits that will accrue from their effective implementation (relative to the costs of not taking any action at all).

- Outline clearly what actions need to be taken as a result of the recommendations, and by whom. It might also be important to refer briefly to the wider implications of the findings.

- Ask someone to read a draft of the report and to provide constructive criticism from the perspective of the reader.

WRITING A REPORT SUMMARY

EXERCISE 6

One of the hardest aspects of report writing is the need to be brief and concise. Read a report that someone else has written, preferably a report on an evaluation study. Produce an executive summary using a maximum of 500 words. Imagine that the summary is designed to be more widely circulated than the report itself and to a more varied audience.

TRANSLATING DATA: THE USE OF VISUAL MEDIA

Numerical results are best presented in descriptive form rather than as an abstract set of inferential statistical tests. Few people will be interested in say, *t*-test or ANOVA details. The majority will prefer to examine the data in its more concrete, descriptive form (e.g. the mean difference between outcomes obtained pre-event and post-event). To maximize the presentational impact of descriptive data you will need to consider how to select and use various forms of visual media.

USES OF TABLES, FIGURES AND GRAPHS

The aim of communication by visual media is to present the essential facts of a situation in a simple form. Tabular presentation is one way of presenting statistical facts in order to trace patterns in the data but there are many instances where a graphic presentation (i.e. figures and graphs) is more appropriate. Tables, figures and graphs can be used:

- as *signposts* to provide structure
- for *illustration* or *emphasis*
- to spell out *key words* or *main points*
- to provide lasting *impressions*
- to provide graphics which help *simplify* explanations
- to *clarify relationships*
- to *vary* the pace.

CHOICE OF VISUAL MEDIUM

Your choice of visual medium depends on the degree of formality of the presentation. In an oral presentation the use of an OHP (overhead projector) is more formal than use of a flip-chart, for example. High quality acetates can be professionally produced using various computer graphics or using lettering aids (e.g. dry transfer lettering or stencils) whereas the quality of a flip-chart depends on handwriting ability. Blackboard chalk can be messy on the hands and cleaning blackboards or whiteboards can prove awkward during a formal presentation. Handout material can be provided but needs to be structured into the presentation systematically.

TYPES OF TABLES AND FIGURES

FIGURES
A figure might be used to outline the timetable of the project as in
the sideways bar chart shown in Figure 6.1.

Figure 6.1 Timetable of project activities

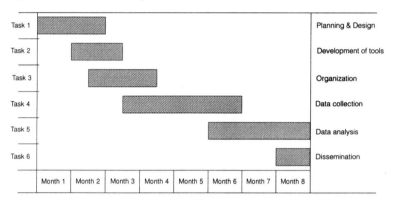

Numerical results can also be presented in a table, for example the
pre-event and post-event test results for children's reading scores
shown below. An interpretation of these scores can be found in
Chapter 5, page 86.

Table 6.1 Reading scores of children aged 6–7 years before and after
a teaching intervention

Pre-intervention	Post-intervention	Difference (pre-post)
4.5	7.8	3.3
4.7	4.6	–0.1
4.2	6.8	2.6
4.9	5.0	0.1
3.6	6.1	2.5
5.1	4.0	–1.1
3.8	4.7	0.9
30.8	39.0	8.2
4.4	5.6	1.2

A form of table known as a bar chart can be used to document frequencies or percentages. Findings are more instantly accessible in this form and facilitate comparison. In the example data used are derived from the case study involving the observation of care workers in their ways of interacting with children with learning difficulties. Information is conveyed by the *length* of the vertical bar.

Figure 6.2 Bar chart showing the co-occurrence of certain carer and child behaviours

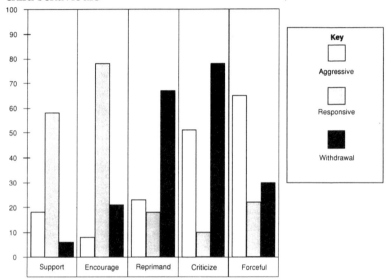

Five categories of care worker behaviour are represented on the horizontal axis. The length of the three bars depicted within each category of care worker behaviour represents the frequency of occurrence (0–100) of three types of child behaviour or reaction to the care worker. The key alongside provides an indicator of the type of behaviour represented by each of the three different bars. From this it can be seen that the frequency of aggression on the part of the child is substantially higher when care workers are 'forceful' or 'critical' in their way of handling the child. Child 'withdrawal' is especially likely to occur if care workers are 'critical' or 'reprimanding'. By contrast, when care workers are 'encouraging' or 'supportive' the child is more likely to be 'responsive' than either 'aggressive' or 'withdrawing'. The bar chart clearly helps in describing and explaining these kinds of findings to an audience. Some points to note include:

- The bars can be presented in horizontal or vertical form.
- The scale must be chosen so that all data can appear easily in the space available. The largest piece of data should use almost the whole scale.
- Bars should be the same width since only the length of the bar is used to make comparisons across the data. Assume a scale of 1cm per 5 points on a scale (or 5 occurrences). If you wish to represent 30 points on the scale (or 30 occurrences) then the bar should be $30/5 = 6$cm long.
- Shading, colouring or cross-hatching can be helpful in differentiating between bars.
- Positive and negative findings can be represented in the same bar chart by presenting bars either above or below zero.

GRAPHS

A graph is a pictorial representation of the data which can be used to show the relationship between two or more variables. Two lines called axes are drawn at right angles to one another which serve as the coordinates of the graph: the horizontal axis (or *abscissa*) is used to plot the '**causal**' variable whilst the vertical axis (or *ordinate*) is used to plot the '**outcome**' measure. Two or more lines can be put on any one graph so long as their relationship to each other is clear and they are well differentiated (e.g. different line patterns can

Figure 6.3 Skill ratings of care workers in handling instances of violence

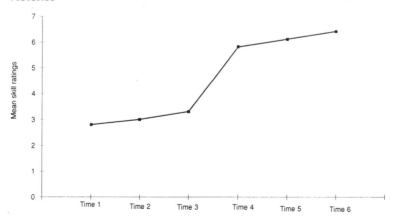

be used). Diagrammatic figures provide more scope than tables for depicting relationships between one event and another and to trace patterns of change of one or more groups over time. The examples highlight the use of graphs using data reproduced from the examples in Chapter 5.

Figure 6.3 shows the substantial improvement made by care workers in handling instances of child violence after receiving a training intervention on 'control and restraint'. The graph can also be used to make the following points: a) that a small and insignificant rise in ability to handle violent children was evident before the intervention; b) that the intervention significantly 'interrupted' this trend in the data by facilitating rapid improvement; and c) that the benefits of the training were maintained and consolidated over time. Sceptics would find it very hard to dispute the 'benefit' of the intervention on the basis of data presented in this way. The next graph traces changes in two groups over time also using data reproduced from Chapter 5. The main advantage of the graphic presentation of this data is that it illustrates clearly the interaction between *class* and *time*. In other words, the changes observed for Class 1 relative to Class 2 are highlighted against the teaching event they received. Statistical interactions are nearly always best explained in graphic form.

Figure 6.4 Showing mean scores of treatment and comparison group pre- and post-intervention

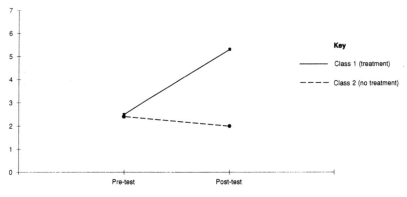

BASIC CONSIDERATIONS IN THE USE OF TABLES AND FIGURES

- Each table and figure must be self-explanatory with a clear and comprehensive title, a key to explain symbols and footnotes to explain certain omissions.
- Each table and figure must indicate the number of cases (i.e. participants) on which the information is based.
- Discuss the key findings shown in the table, or represented in the figure, in the text.
- Provide instructions for how to read a graph.
- Figures usually convey less information than a table, in which case both may need to be included for the same set of data.
- Ensure all the tables and figures are numbered throughout the report. It is usual to number tables and figures in a separate sequence (Table 1, Table 2 etc; Figure 1, Figure 2 etc.). If there are several tables and figures an index of these will be helpful at the beginning of the report.
- Pay particular attention to the use of scale when producing figures. The judicious use of scale can help emphasize a certain finding as in the figure below, i.e. it can reveal a starker trend of change or difference than appears from simply staring at a numerical table. At the same time, scale can be used in a misleading and thus inappropriate way as in Figure 6.6. (Note that Figures 6.5 and 6.6 present the same data.)

Figure 6.5 An illustration of the use of scale for emphasising trends in data

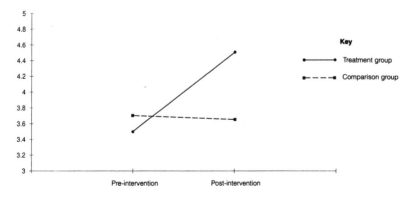

Figure 6.6 An illustration of misleading use of scale in depicting data

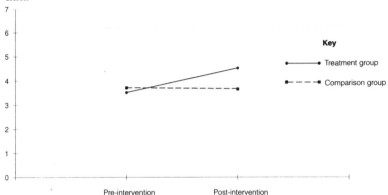

TRANSLATING DATA INTO GRAPHIC FORM

EXERCISE 7

Use the data tables below to produce a set of graphics which depict discernible patterns in the best way.

1. A table showing mean levels of commitment to quality principles and practice of shop floor employees from two industrial organizations before and after the introduction of an employee participation programme. (Scores out of 7; the higher the score the greater the commitment expressed.)

	Pre-employee participation	Post-employee participation	
	3 months prior	3 months after	12 months after
Employee participation	3.6	4.1	6.3
No employee participation	4.0	4.6	4.8

2. The following table refers to data reported in Chapter 5. It reports the number of women who attended for breast screening according to the type of marketing pamphlet they received.

	Pamphlet 1	**Pamphlet 2**	**Row totals**
Attended	56	34	90
Not attend	28	49	77
Column total	84	83	**Grand total** = 167

Chapter Seven

Putting the Findings into Practice

PROBLEMS IN USING EVALUATION FINDINGS

This chapter is necessary because there are often problems which arise in implementing any recommendations that follow from the findings of an evaluation. It identifies the types of problems that might emerge and examines how they can be handled. Before pursuing that, it is worth mentioning that not all evaluations generate recommendations. An evaluation can be geared simply to offering an assessment of current provisions, practices and procedures without suggesting what changes might be needed. The problem then becomes one of deriving recommendations from the findings of the evaluator. If the responsibility of the evaluator stops with the assessment, translation of the findings into recommendations for new provisions, practices and procedures can be left to the people 'at the coal face' i.e. to those who are directly involved. Of course, where the evaluator is also directly involved this separation of responsibility becomes rather irrelevant.

Deriving recommendations from an evaluation may not be very easy. An evaluation will usually tell you whether the thing evaluated is doing what you wish it to do. If it is, then the recommendation may be simple: leave it alone. If it is not, then the problems start. The evaluation can either pinpoint what is going wrong – i.e. things that need changing – or not. If it does, then either it may offer clues to how they might be changed, or not. An evaluation *per se* rarely produces clear-cut suggestions for rectifying a provision, practice or procedure. Just because it shows one thing is not succeeding, it does not necessarily show what other thing might succeed better. An evaluation has to be carefully designed if it is to reveal what alternatives might be preferable. In a majority of cases the evaluation will indicate only that the current state of affairs must be changed. This is, of course, a recommendation in itself- i.e. the recommendation is: change. The recommendation is not, however, change in a particular direction. Merely complying with the recommendation to change may be difficult but setting in train a mechanism for establishing the direction of change is likely to be infinitely more difficult. Anyone engaging in or commissioning an evaluation has to consider how the direction of change will be determined – preferably before the evaluation is done. When thinking about introducing change it is useful to visualize the 'evaluation cycle' depicted in the model below.

Figure 7.1 The Evaluation Cycle

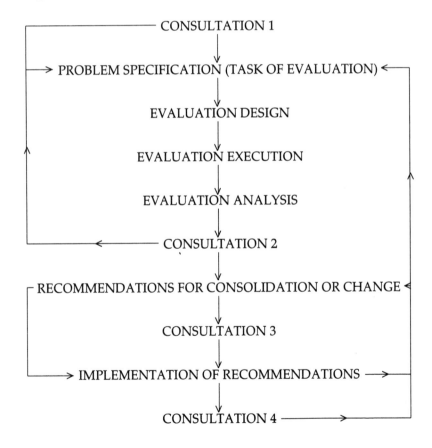

The evaluation cycle assumes that the process starts with some sort of consultation. This first consultation need not be formal but involves basically sampling the views of others to come to an opinion about the purpose of evaluation. Even where self-evaluation is concerned, some consultation may occur. Consultation 1 allows for the specification of the task for evaluation. This then leads to the design, execution and analysis of the evaluation, factors which have been considered in detail in other chapters. In the complete cycle, analysis should be followed by consultation 2. This consultation is designed to allow the range of alternative potential changes to be considered and weighed before reaching a recommendation for a particular change. The production of a recommendation should be followed by consultation 3 which will consider the practicalities of how to implement the chosen change. Actual implementation is followed by a final consultation 4 which allows unanticipated difficulties in implementation to be assessed and removed. This complete cycle can be abridged at a number of junctures as indicated; most of these short cuts involve dropping a consultative phase. The evaluation cycle illustrates that recommendations for change are not an integral part of the body of the evaluation. If they are to be generated an appropriate phase structure for the evaluation must be planned from the outset.

Having made the point that evaluation does not inevitably produce recommendations, what follows in this chapter will focus on the problems that occur when they are forthcoming. Assuming recommendations are derived from an evaluation, the nature and extent of the problems in their implementation will depend upon three key variables: what the findings are and the recommendations they generate; the position and power of the evaluator; and the context, particularly the organizational climate, in which the evaluation occurred. Crudely, the difficulty in implementing evaluation recommendations increases when:

- The recommendations are regarded as criticizing current provisions, practices or procedures.

- The recommendations are complex (for instance, contained one within another or contingent upon one another).

- The recommendations are unanticipated.

- The recommendations require changes which are either large or diverse.

- The evaluator has little personal power or little persuasive power.

- The evaluator has little position power or low support from those with such position power.

- The organizational climate has succumbed to 'change fatigue'. This occurs after an organization experiences repeated demands to change in a short period of time. Personnel can become unresponsive to the need to change even where the specific change may be positively regarded; the mere possibility of change becomes anathema.

Obviously, some of these barriers against implementation can be removed by taking care in the way recommendations are introduced and explained. Others are less easily pinpointed. These issues of evaluator power and organizational climate need to be considered in more detail.

BASES OF EVALUATOR POWER

The foundations of the evaluator's power to implement recommendations vary according to their position in the organization. Certainly, they are different for evaluators who are external to the organization from those who are internal.

EXTERNAL EVALUATORS

If you, as the evaluator, are not part of the organization under evaluation, your power can come from being recognized as an expert. Such acknowledgement of your credentials is often vital in persuading others to accept your recommendations for change. Your 'expert power' can be enhanced by emphasizing your independence. By laying claim to producing recommendations untarnished by self-interest, the external evaluator can sometimes persuade an organization to listen whereas an internal evaluator inevitably is assumed to be involved, therefore biased, and consequently can be disregarded. External evaluators can also bolster their power to enact change by making it clear that they have been commissioned by, and have the backing of, people in the organization with authority. Of course, as soon as external evaluators have recourse to an internal authority to support their power, their claim to independence evaporates.

The idea that the external evaluator is independent is clearly a myth. In accepting a commission the evaluator steps inside the system to be evaluated – maybe not to the extent that habitual inmates are within it but enough to lose independence. In recognizing this, it becomes important also to acknowledge that this loss of independence does not necessarily result in any erosion of objectivity. The expert evaluator can operate according to criteria and with techniques that ensure objectivity (as far as it is ever possible in social research) and guard against any accidental or deliberate fudging of data. The problem at the point of implementation often lies in persuading others that losing independence does not mean abandoning objectivity. Maintaining the advantages of being external to the system and being an expert in evaluation once implementation is attempted depends upon being accepted as 'fair'. Such a reputation for fairness can only be gained through executing the evaluation itself in a manner which is seen to be valid and reliable, and most importantly, morally justifiable.

INTERNAL EVALUATORS

Evaluators who are internal to the organization usually have two possible sources of power. First, their position in the organization, which has presumably condoned the evaluation, may offer them a platform from which to implement recommendations. Second, their previous record of successful innovation in the organization may lead to support for any change they recommend. Essentially, these two sources of power are authority and respect.

Individual authority and respect yield quite different results in different types of organization. A rather naïve but nevertheless instructive tripartite classification of organizational structures is sometimes used to denote these types which distinguishes between authoritarian, democratic and *laissez-faire* organizations. An **authoritarian organization** has a strict hierarchy; decisions are taken by those higher in the hierarchy and imposed on those below in a cascade of control. A **democratic organization** allows everyone equal rights in determining decisions but once a course has been decided by the majority everyone is expected to adhere to it. A *laissez-faire* **organization** establishes overall goals (through consensus or imposition from the more powerful) but within broad bounds allows individuals independence of decision-making. Clearly, having authority in an authoritarian structure is likely to lead to effective implementation of evaluation recommendations. Inspiring respect in either a democratic or a *laissez-faire* organization would maximize chances of successful implementation.

Return to Figure 7.1 for a moment. The authoritarian structure is likely to remove the consultation phases. The democratic structure is likely to use these phases rigorously. The laissez-faire structure is most likely to include them but not use their outputs systematically. With or without consultation, the type of organizational structure will influence the tactics which can be used in implementing change. This is considered further in the discussion of tactics.

Whatever the basis of evaluator power, except in the most thoroughgoing authoritarian systems, some compromise in the implementation of evaluation recommendations is likely. Implementation is often a matter of successive approximation, with changes being introduced piecemeal over time. Some of the methods described below help to speed up this process. The key to all of this is that the problems of implementation should not be addressed as an afterthought. If you have designed the evaluation well, you will have anticipated the problems of implementation and they will be reduced by the fact that the evaluation is:

- seen to be relevant to an important question i.e. not silly or pointless

- known to have been designed appropriately

- recognized as having been executed with precision

- understood to have been analysed properly

- felt to have been presented effectively.

The emphasis is clearly upon how the evaluation itself is regarded by the people who must accept the change. The essential ingredient here is that you have to have fought any public relations battles right from the start. It may be too late to think about explaining and justifying the evaluation to your public (whoever they might be) only when you want to introduce changes. The public has to be primed to accept the changes that emanate from the evaluation by being led to accept the evaluation itself.

WHAT CAN GO WRONG IN PUTTING FINDINGS INTO PRACTICE?

Even the best laid plans go astray sometimes and there are some very common routes to disaster. The box opposite summarizes the most frequent difficulties.

COMMON DIFFICULTIES IN IMPLEMENTATION

Problem 1: Premature revelation of findings

Findings can be revealed prematurely for a number of reasons. Most simply it can occur as the result of an error in judgement on the part of the evaluator. More frequently, it can occur when the person commissioning the evaluation insists that findings are presented to meet some deadline not negotiated with the evaluator. Sometimes, premature revelation is precipitated through agitation by people who are anxious about the evaluation or antipathetic towards it.

Premature revelation is problematic when it results in findings being presented before they have been thoroughly analysed or their implications for changes properly assessed. It is particularly awkward when it permits opponents more time to organize their defences against the planned change.

Answers: Timing and Openness

Timetabling the revelation of findings from the outset. of the design of the programme is vital. This timetable should encompass both the evaluator and anyone commissioning the evaluation. The initial timetable may be modified as the work progresses but this should be done only after assessing the likely consequences for the implementation of change.

Pressure from opponents for premature revelation of findings must be expected. Phased openness is a great defence. This involves working out how much can be said about the evaluation at each of its phases without hazarding its success. This information is given at the scheduled times to maximize the actual and apparent openness of the evaluation. Such a tactic militates against unnecessary secrecy which can be misinterpreted and cause resentment at the point of implementation.

Problem 2: Campaigns to discredit findings

Evaluations are not infrequently subjected to campaigns which are designed to discredit them. In evaluation it is dangerous to discount conspiracy theories. Opponents commonly use a number of tactics to discredit an evaluation. First, they may try to discredit the work directly – challenging the adequacy of the design, execution or analysis. Such critiques can deviate from strictly factual accounts of what you did. The opponents' representation of your methods may not be accurate and the critique is focused on their representation not on what you actually did. The misrepresentations, not surprisingly, allow somewhat greater room for their attack. Second, they may try to discredit the evaluation indirectly: by association. This might entail telling tales of previous evaluations you have done which had dire effects (for

— *continued* —

continued –

example, job losses, introduction of poor services, harm to clients, etc). It might involve stories of erstwhile co-workers you have had who are known to have made errors. It might involve associating you with some other evaluation process that went on in the past, that you had nothing to do with, but which went badly wrong.

Discrediting by association, as is evident from this short list of examples, has many tactics. The third type of discrediting tactic involves attacking the evaluation on ethical grounds. There are again a number of variants on this tactic. On one hand, the process of evaluation itself can be castigated as unethical. This might be viable if, for example, information gathering had breached data protection laws or privacy norms or misled people about the purpose of the study, and so on. On the other hand, the product of the evaluation can be criticized as unethical. This might occur if the recommendations involve a moral dimension.

Typically, for example, any recommendation which results in the very young or the very old losing some benefit will result in moral outrage and this will be fostered by opponents. The production of recommendations after an evaluation often involves making moral judgements in the sense that costs and benefits to the different people involved in the proposed changes have to be weighed and the scales used are balanced on moral imperatives. This means that the majority of evaluation recommendations are open to moral critique at some level.

Answers: Good quality information and 'tenacious responsiveness'

Campaigns designed to discredit are very difficult to rebut. They are more difficult to mount if the evaluator ensures that good information is given about the study right from the start. Again this harks back to the concept of 'phased openness'. However, good information does not simply mean well-timed information. It also means well-organized, well-presented and properly disseminated information.

The potential for attacks on moral grounds means that it helps if the evaluator is ethically 'squeaky clean'. Obviously the evaluation itself must use methods that are morally defensible. The recommendations, if they have a moral dimension, can be defended against damage from any ethical bombshell if the evaluator sets up a system of 'tenacious responsiveness'. This entails responding quickly and persistently to any moral criticism. It may not silence the critics but it will show that the recommendations offered are not presented without consideration of the counter-arguments. Silence and barricades in the face of moral onslaught are poor defences.

– *continued*

— continued — –

Problem 3: Challenges on interpretation of findings

Evaluators often find themselves faced with challenges about their interpretation of findings and thus of their recommendations. The challenges are motivated by the desire to resist change but can have their origin in genuine problems in making sense of the findings. Many people have grave difficulties in understanding the logic of the scientific method and find statistical estimates of probability anathema. The rhetoric of control groups, time series, and probabilities of 0.001 are incomprehensible to the majority of the people who will be affected by an evaluation. Such people may challenge the interpretation on any number of grounds, often illogically. Perhaps of more concern are those who understand the methods partially and will generate spurious, but on the surface logical, challenges. These are more dangerous since they muddy the waters further for those who are ignorant of the facts but willing to learn.

Answers: **Avoid technical justifications and give graphic examples**

Where the challenge on interpretation emanates from a someone who clearly understands the methods you used, a technical justification is appropriate. However, in the cases described above where ignorance and partial ignorance prevail, the technical justification can simply result in further problems. In this situation, technical debates should be avoided. The best way to persuade a critic that your interpretation is correct is often to present a graphic illustration of what you found. The illustration can be contrived, it does not have to be an actual example derived from your data. It can be the distillation of a series of cases in the data set. This also has the advantage of maintaining confidentiality when this has been promised in individual cases.

SELF-EVALUATION AND CHANGE

In earlier chapters, the value of self-evaluation has been discussed. It is appropriate therefore to consider here the peculiar problems of implementing recommendations for change resulting from self-evaluation. Before continuing, try the self-assessment exercise below (*Exercise 8*). This is designed to make you think about how much you listen to yourself.

HOW GOOD ARE YOU AT LISTENING TO YOURSELF?

EXERCISE 8

Answer the questions by ticking the appropriate column. Answer quickly; do not ponder the question too carefully. Your first reactions are what is required.

In answering you might find it easier to focus on a single area of your life which you might want to evaluate and then change (for example: your behaviour towards someone in your family, your consumption of specific foods or your execution of particular tasks at work). You could even do the assessment several times, considering in turn a different area of your life. It is undoubtedly true that the same person will differ in his or her responsiveness to self-evaluation recommendations according to which aspect of their life is involved.

Answer the following with a YES or NO:

	YES	NO
1. Are you more likely to change because you think you should than because other people say you should?	☐	☐
2. Do you find you live up to your own resolutions for changing yourself?	☐	☐
3. Do you find it hard just to think about changing yourself?	☐	☐
4. Do you enjoy working out how you should bring about change in yourself?	☐	☐
5. Do you find your attempts to change are thwarted by other people?	☐	☐
6. Do you catch yourself persuading yourself that change is pointless for you?	☐	☐
7. Do you believe that even if it is painful, change can be worthwhile?	☐	☐
8. Do you find that you are pretty sure what changes you need to make in yourself?	☐	☐
9. Do you start to implement changes and then lose interest?	☐	☐
10. Do you sometimes pretend to yourself that a change has been made when really you know it has not?	☐	☐

continued

continued —

Scoring the self-assessment: Score 1 for answering YES to each of questions 1, 2, 4, 7, and 8. Score 1 for answering NO to questions 3, 5, 6, 9 and 10. Sum your score. The higher the score, the more you will acknowledge your own belief that you need to change.

Doing this exercise may have highlighted for you why implementing recommendations for change after a self-evaluation is no bed of rose petals (we do not say roses, since the whole rose has thorns and implementation is rather thorny!). Basically it is difficult because:

- understanding of the required change may be missing

- motivation may be absent

- skills may be absent, i.e. the abilities necessary to introduce change

- support from others may be absent

- situational constraints may be present, e.g. lack of resources or time.

RESISTANCE TO ORGANIZATIONAL CHANGE

Changing yourself may be difficult; changing organizations is usually more difficult. The processes which operate to slow, subvert or prevent personal change are all present – writ large, when dealing with conglomerates of people inhabiting established systems with traditions and histories of conflict.

UNDERSTANDING THE CHANGE

The organization may have no clear understanding of what change is required. Even when told, the organization can fail to comprehend. For instance, in one case, an evaluator made the recommendation to a hospital management committee that catering facilities would be improved if weekend provisions were radically overhauled and subcontracting to a private firm of caterers, explored. The hospital management committee took this as a recommendation to privatize all catering facilities and radically reduce services at weekends. Here there is an evident gap between the transmitted recommendation for change and its received form. Just as radio messages can be blocked, attenuated or amplified by environmental factors, recommendations can be distorted by the organizational environment. The distortion can be wilful or coincidental. If it is wilful the evaluator stands little chance of controlling it. At that point, however, the evaluator has to ask who has real responsibility for the implementation of the recommendations. Somewhere along the line the evaluator has to acknowledge that implementation is the responsibility of the organization. If the evaluator is part of the organization this escape from responsibility is barred. But if the evaluator is external to the organization then the decision to withdraw can be legitimate. As long as every step has been taken to ensure accurate understanding of the recommendations, the evaluator can regard wilful misinterpretation as someone else's problem.

Organizations are particularly good at amplifying the risks associated with change. This distortion serves a purpose – it is not random or accidental. It protects organizational inertia and it offers an apparently rational explanation for the resistance to change. This amplification of risk is often generated by an informal process involving rumour and gossip; the 'rumour machine' is present in any organization. This mechanism takes a piece of information and, during its passage between people (in successive revisions at each transmission to a new person), simultaneously strips the information of subtlety or complexity and imbues it with drama or intensity. After the rumour machine treatment, a sophisticated series of propositions for organizational change will be reshaped into major, radical disruption. Rumour operates to simplify and to dramatize. Sometimes this process eventually will produce a story which is more complicated than the original but the phase of simplification is normally an essential precursor. Rumour is no guardian of truth: it can result in complete fiction being incorporated into the story.

The only tactic that the evaluator can apply to guard against the ravages of rumour is to promulgate a good, simple information flow. This has been a central tenet throughout this book. The implementation of recommendations from an evaluation is infinitely easier if all concerned are properly informed. Even good information will not preclude some rumour-mongering but it will minimize the possibility of negative developments taking hold.

Aggressive publicity about what is really happening cuts the ground from under the rumour machine.

One further point should be made about rumour. You can learn a lot about what worries an organization by listening to the rumours which circulate and watching how they change over time. Rumour is a good subsidiary source of information for the evaluator who wishes to understand how to implement change. It indicates which areas are most sensitive. Also, if traced to its significant sources, it can reveal who are the informal opinion leaders in the organization. Therefore, rumour should not be dismissed merely as some sort of 'noise in the system'.

MOTIVATING THE CHANGE

Just like individuals, organizations may resist change because they are demotivated. The central factor here is that to bring about change an organization, particularly its key managers (but also other personnel if the change is to be accepted and fully influence practice), must believe that it will yield rewards. Recommendations for change are more motivating if they can be framed with clear rewards attached. The evaluator might wish to consider indicating the rewards resulting from the changes, not just for senior management, or those immediately concerned with the changes, but also for people affected indirectly. Those people peripheral to the change will then see the rewards they will get if they support it and some further portion of organizational inertia thereby is removed.

OVERCOMING THE STRESS OF CHANGE

Organizations engaged in significant change experience stress. Change which is extensive (i.e. affecting a large part of the organization) or extended (i.e. continuing over a considerable time period) is particularly stressful. The stress of extensive or extended change can be best assuaged by presenting a coherent plan to members of the organization from the beginning. Changes which are piecemeal, iterative and apparently unrelated or unpredictable are most threatening and disruptive.

In some ways, organizations which are stressed react like stressed individuals – hardly surprising when the stressed organization is comprised of stressed individuals. People who are stressed exhibit a range of reactions varying in severity according to the extent of the stress:

- inability to concentrate and attend to new information
- failures in retrieval of information previously memorized
- emotionality, particularly a tendency to irascibility and depression
- lack of self-confidence
- disruptions in the performance of normal activities
- breakdowns in the ability to communicate effectively.

Organizations which are stressed show similar symptoms. These become particularly manifest in the context of decision-making. Decision-makers in an organization under stress will tend to fail to assimilate all information relevant to making a good decision. They will foreclose on options before considering all the alternatives or will stick to decisions even after they are shown to be weak. They may become hostile towards anyone who contradicts them, refusing to listen to external expert advice. Or they will be slow to consider what other people might think about their decisions and will stereotype anyone outside their immediate circle as an enemy who is not to be trusted and is probably out to undermine their authority. Introducing change in such a climate of aggressive suspicion clearly is not easy.

It is worth considering the possibility of introducing a system of stress reduction strategies when implementing change. These can be extensions of those used at the individual level. Problems with decision-making groups can be moderated by encouraging a change in the normal procedures of the group. For instance, if you are a member of a group and have some power, over time you can introduce an expectation that people who make any recommendation for action will present both the pros and cons of their position, thus inculcating a norm of self-criticism and reflection. You can introduce external experts to offer advice on a routine basis. This means that when the group faces a crisis, expert advice usually is regarded as more acceptable and relevant. You can allow time for the group to take 'time-outs' during decision-making. These can be literal – i.e. imposing a period after an initial decision is made to its execution – or they can be more metaphorical, allowing people time to play with the problem without demanding immediate answers.

An external evaluator may not be able to modify the effects of stress such that it transforms the willingness of an organization to countenance change. To do so, they would need authoritative internal support. From the external evaluator's point of view the best way to control the effects of organizational stress is not to arouse it in the first place. By introducing plans for change which are clearly explained the evaluator will minimize the stress induced. It is, therefore, the responsibility of the evaluator to explain any such recommendation in the clearest possible terms. This entails providing:

1. The details of the changes broken into component parts – who is involved, what they must do differently, etc.
2. The timetable for change, i.e. when each component of the changes should occur.
3. The benefits of change for everyone either directly or indirectly affected, i.e. the motivational factor.

Additionally, the evaluator might be expected to provide management with clues as to how the package of changes should be presented to other members of the organization. This might include a series of slogans summarizing the changes needed plus some suggestions as to how the benefits could be highlighted and memorized. For instance, an evaluator might advise management that members of the organization would be more likely to make the changes if they had an opportunity to discuss any problems, perhaps in small groups beforehand. An example of how this works might help.

A construction company found that it was experiencing an unacceptably large number of accidents in its workforce due to slackness in the adherence to safety guidelines. The evaluator looked at procedures and suggested a number of changes in the way the workforce was trained in the safety routines and some modification of the guidelines themselves. Management accepted that these changes were necessary. The evaluator, knowing that safety procedures are frequently subverted or ignored by workers, suggested that key members of the workforce – team leaders – should be brought together, have the new procedures described to them and be allowed to express any doubts that they had about changes. This allowed transition to new operating practices to be made without those involved misunderstanding the motive for them and with the teams knowing precisely what was expected. The workers also had some input because it emerged in the training sessions that a further change in equipment was necessary to optimize the effect of the changes. The outcome was a reduction in accidents and an increase in productivity. The evaluation more than paid for itself and the stress of change was minimized.

This is really an example of the way in which the evaluator can provide the skills necessary to bring about change. An organization may be motivated to change and may understand what is required but may not know how to bring it about. The evaluator can then become the real agent of change, masterminding the whole process. This is, however, rare. Most organizations once informed as to the direction of change required will have mechanisms for bringing it about themselves. Organizations usually have too many eccentricities in their procedures for an evaluator to be able to operate effectively as a director of change.

SUPPORT FOR CHANGE

In the same way that an individual will look for support in coping with change, organizations will seek support. If the organization is large enough it will be subject to the vagaries of media support – or condemnation. Most large organizations are nowadays sensitive to media attention. Evaluations need to take the media into account since their external reaction will influence the process of implementation. An evaluator who is aware of media reactions will be ready to:

- Provide clear crisp summaries of the design and results of the evaluation.

- Provide comprehensible summaries of recommendations (again, preferably with graphic illustrations).

These should not be given directly to outside agencies such as the media but to the management of the organization concerned for it to give out later on. The evaluator who does this minimizes the chances of the organization being misrepresented.

It is always worth bearing in mind the fact that the media have their own agenda. This includes entertainment as well as information. You might expect your message to be distorted by the media if it does not satisfy their objectives.

Organizations will not introduce changes when they feel that the media might pillory them for doing so. This means that an evaluator does need to understand the media implications of any recommendations for change. As always, the temptation is to let the organization take the decision about the media viability of any change. There is, however, an alternative. This entails offering the organization a way of presenting the change in a 'media-friendly' fashion. Again, this is beyond the responsibility normally required in an evaluation but it is, nevertheless, a serious consideration if you are an internal evaluator who has a personal investment in the changes. Unfortunately, dealing with the media is beyond the scope of this book. Suffice it to say here that the evaluator who ignores the media, ignores the future.

CONCLUSION: THE RHETORIC OF EVALUATION

This book has described some of the central tenets of evaluation methods. The conscientious reader should now know enough to conduct an evaluation, analyse it, present its findings and set about implementing any changes suggested. If there are two fundamental messages that this book contains, they are first that if you build evaluation into your provision, practices and procedures you build in change and, second, having facts is not enough to engender change. The prospective evaluator who learns these lessons has learned both the power and the limitation of the science of evaluation.

INDEX

Absolute standard 33
activity evaluation 3
analysis
　of data 77–97
　of variance (ANOVA) 93–95
appraisal 10–11
attitude scales 64–66
audience analysis 100
authoritarian organization 129–130

'Before-and-after' design 34–39
　data analysis 86–89
　time series variation 36–37
　with controls 37–39, 92–95
behaviour recording 51–53
benefits of evaluation 11–13
　case study 13–14

Case studies
　planning exercise 103–105
　social services team: costs and
　　benefits 13–14
causal variable 121
central tendency 80
change
　motivating 137
　overcoming stress 137–140
　resistance 135–140
　self-evaluation 133–135
　support 140–141
　understanding 135–136
Chi-Square 90
class 94–95
coding
　criteria 52
　scheme for data 75
collecting data 47–76
conceptual models 79
condemnation 4
confidence limits 87–88
convenience sample 83
costs of evaluation 11–13
　case study 13–14
cycle of evaluation 126–127

Data
　analysis 77–97
　coding scheme 75
　collection 47–76
　describing and summarizing
　　80–83
　differences 84–86
　handling model 78–79

interpretation 90–92
　from interviews 71
　quantifying 47
　translation 118–124
　variation 81–83
decision tree for test selection 97
degrees of freedom 87
democratic organization 129–130
designing an evaluation 31–46
designs
　'before-and-after' 34–39
　'now' 33–34
　'now and then' 39–40
　optimizing solution 40–44
detached observation 55–57
differences
　testing significance 84–86
　true 87
dissemination of information
　98–105

Ethics 28–30
evaluation
　before the event 20
　costs and benefits 11–13
　cycle 126–127
　design 31–46
　ethics 28–30
　findings 125–140
　initial assessment 15
　introduction 2–3
　of outcome 24–27
　of process 24–25
　purposes 4
　relationships 6–7, 43–44
　in retrospect 45–46
　rhetoric 141
　scope 3–4
　strategy 46
　tactics 47–76
　when to conduct 16–18
evaluators 42–44
　bases of power 128–130
　external 128–129
　internal 129–130
evidence
　obtaining 47–76
　scoring, interpreting and
　　analysing 54
　secondary sources 73–76
　sources 48
expected frequencies 90
explanation 96–97

external evaluation 6–7, 43
external evaluators 128–129

Filtering 18
findings
   interpretation 90–92
   presentation 98–124
   problems 125–128, 130–133
   putting into practice 125–141
frequencies 90

Gain score analysis 78
graphs 121–124

Implementation difficulties 131–133
imposed evaluation 6–7, 43
improvement 4
independent component 92
inferences 18
information
   dissemination 98–105
   and intelligence 18–19
   presentation 110
initial evaluation assessment 15
interaction effect 92
internal evaluation 6–7, 43
internal evaluators 129–130
interpretation of findings 90–92
interviews 67–73
   conducting 70–71
   defining purpose 69
   pros and cons 72–73
   schedule 70
   timetabling 69–70
   transcription 71
invited evaluation 6–7, 43
involved observation 55–57

Laissez-faire organization 129–130
level of event 41
Likert scale 64–66
linkage 18

Main effect 94–95
management information systems
   (MIS) 27–28
mapping evaluation strategy 31–46
meta-analysis 22–24
motivating change 137
Museum Director's problem 26

Non-participatory evaluation 6–8,
   44
'now' design 33–34
'now and then' design 39–40
   data ananysis 89–90

Objectives
   evaluation 4
observation
   conducting 54
   detached and involved 55 57
   procedure 49–55
   pros and cons 56–57
   schedule 50–51
observers
   selection and training 53
obtained frequencies 90
oral presentation 105–115
organizational change 135–141
organizational structure evaluation
   4
outcome evaluation 24–27
   measure 121

Participants
   preparation 53–54
participatory evaluation 6–8, 44
patterning 18
personnel evaluation 3
pinpoint selection 42
planning case study 103–105
pointless evaluation 18–19
prediction 96
preparation of participants
   53–54
presentation
   of findings 98–124
   planning case study 103–105
   written and oral 105–115
problems with findings 125–128,
   130–133
process evaluation 24–25
process factors 96
programme evaluation 4–5

Quantifying data 47
questionnaires 58–67
   development 59–61
   pros and cons 67
   service evaluation 62–63
questions
   posing 19–20
quota sample 83
quota sampling 42

Random sample 42
range 82
recognition 18
recording behaviour 51–53
records
   authenticity 74

availability 73
behaviour 51–53
content analysis 74–75
related measures 88
related t-test 88
relationships
   between evaluator and evaluated
     6–8
   investigation 79
repeated measure component 92
reports
   structure 116
   summary 117
   writing 115–117
resistance to change 135–140
resources
   provision evaluation 3

Sample mean 80
sampling 41–42, 83–86
   errors 84
   strategy 69–70
sampling plan 50
   production 58–59
   for record collection 73
scale of event 41
secondary sources of evidence
   73–76
selective transcription 74–75

self-evaluation 8–11
   change 133–135
semantic differential 64–65
simulation 20–22
standard deviation 82
stress of change 137–140
structuring 18
   formal presentation 110–111
survey timetable 58–59

Tables and figures 118–124
targets
   initial design 27–28
test selection 97
time 94–95
   sampling 50
time-series 36–37, 88–89
transcription
   of interviews 71
   selective 74–75
true difference 87

Validation 4
variance analysis 93–95
variation in data 81–83
visual media 118–124

Writing the report 115–117
written presentation 105–107

FURTHER READING

Asher, H. B. (1983). *Causal Modelling*. London: Sage.

Berry & Feldman (1980). *Multiple Regression in Practice*. London: Sage.

Breakwell, G. M., Hammond, S. and Fife-Schaw, C. R. (Eds.) (1995). *Research Methods in Psychology* (especially Chapter 12 'Questionnaire Design' by C. Fife-Schaw, pp 174–193, and Chapter 24 'Introduction to Multivariate Data Analysis' by S. Hammond, pp 360-385), London: Sage.

Fink, A. (1993). *Evaluation Fundamentals: Guiding Health Programs, Research and Policy*. London: Sage.

Fontana, D. (1989). *Managing Stress*. London: BPS/Routledge.

Green, J. and D'Oliveira, M. (1982). *Learning to Use Statistical Tests in Psychology*. Milton Keynes: Open University Press.

House, E. R. (1993). *Professional Evaluation: Social Impact and Political Consequences*. London: Sage.

Klecka, W. R. (1980). *Discriminant Analysis*. London: Sage.

Krippendorf, K. (1980). *Content Analysis*. London: Sage.

MacRae, A. W. (1994). *Models and Methods for the Behavioural Sciences: Open Learning Unit*. Leicester: BPS Books (British Psychological Society).

MacRae, A. W. (1994). *Describing and Interpreting Data: Open Learning Unit*. Leicester: BPS Books (British Psychological Society).

MacRae, A. W. (1994). *Drawing Inferences from Statistical Data: Open Learning Unit*. Leicester: BPS Books (British Psychological Society).

Mohr, L. B. (1992). *Impact Analysis for Program Evaluation*. London: Sage.

Patton, M. Q. (1990). *Qualitative Evaluation and Research Methods*. (2nd Edition) London: Sage.

Rosenthal, R. (1991). *Meta-Analytic Procedures for Social Research*. (Revised Edition) (Volume 6 in Applied Social Research Methods series) London: Sage.

Rossi, P. H. (1993). *Evaluation: A Systematic Approach*. (5th Edition) London: Sage.

OTHER TITLES IN THE PERSONAL AND PROFESSIONAL DEVELOPMENT SERIES:

Effective Teamwork
Michael West

Teamwork is now a central strategy for most modern organizations, but it presents many challenges and difficulties, and much of what is written about it ignores the underlying research.

This book draws on a wealth of empirical research together with the author's wide experience of working with teams in health care settings, major international organizations (such as IBM and BP) as well as educational institutions.

Using case studies and exercises, this book explores those factors which can prevent and those which promote team effectiveness giving practical and reliable guidelines.

Michael West is co-Director of the Corporate Performance Program of the ESRC Centre for Economic Performance (London School of Economics) and Professor of Work and Organizational Psychology (University of Sheffield).

ISBN: 1 85433 138 8 paperback

OTHER TITLES IN THE PERSONAL AND PROFESSIONAL DEVELOPMENT SERIES:

Coaching for Staff Development
Angela M. Thomas

What is your management style?

This is just one of the many questions the author addresses in demonstrating both organisation and staff development through effective coaching.

This book explores how successful coaching can lead to better working practices, teamwork and job satisfaction, all key elements in obtaining organisational goals. The author also includes a step by step guide to designing coaching programmes and includes self testing exercises to help evaluate both managers and staff.

Written within the realm of psychology in a practical and easy to read style, this is a vital read for all managers with coaching or training responsibilities.

Angela Thomas runs her own management consultancy and conducts coaching and other courses throughout Europe and the States. Previously a lecturer at University of Wales, College of Cardiff, she has extensive experience in office management and training.

ISBN: 1 85433 155 8 paperback